Gertrude Stein
and the Literature
of the Modern
Consciousness

Gertrude Stein and the Literature of the Modern Consciousness

NORMAN WEINSTEIN

Frederick Ungar Publishing Co.
New York

For Dr. Terence Dewsnap
for hearing the music of the words

Acknowledgments

I would like to express my indebtedness to Professors Robert Kelly, Andrews Wanning, and Michael Minihan of the Bard College Literature Department for their various criticisms and enthusiasms; Mr. Aaron Fessler, director, and Mr. Philip Oxley, Reader's Service Librarian of Bard College Library for aid in gathering the most obscure of volumes; to Cathy Kulka, Cathy DeWitt, and Cathy Dalpino for the Promethean tasks of typing, editing, and consoling; to my most patient editors Lina Mainiero and Jean Henrickson.

A most special thanks to Pat, for reasons of the heart, and to all my friends and family who suffered and celebrated these words with me.

Contents

I

Introduction: Gertrude Stein and the Linguistic Revolution

The real metaphysical problem today is the word. The epoch when the writer photographed the life about him with the mechanics of words redolent of the daguerreotype, is happily drawing to a close. The new artist of the word has recognized the autonomy of language and, aware of the twentieth century current toward universality, attempts to hammer out a verbal vision that destroys time and space. . . . Words in modern literature are still being set side by side in the same banal and journalistic fashion as in preceding decades, and the inadequacy of worn-out verbal patterns for our more sensitized nervous systems seems to have struck only a small minority.

—Eugene Jolas[1]

The aim of this book is to examine a range of Gertrude Stein's literary productions in the light of twentieth-century theories of language. Previous studies of Miss Stein's writing, particularly of her "difficult" works, have tended to concentrate on her idiosyncratic uses of words and syntax without placing these experiments in the broader context of modern experimentation with language, its limits, and its levels of usage. Writers such as Joyce, Beckett, and Stein compel us to consider a realm of linguistic possibilities that were utterly unthinkable before our age.

Imagine for a moment confronting a nineteenth-century literary critic—Matthew Arnold perhaps—with Gertrude Stein's portrait of a French society woman:

A little grass. Peal it first it shows clothes that means night gowns hours, loaves feathers, hours, hours, loaves, feathers, feel hours, some more in, little thing, anything, pale letters, principle, principle work show full coal hide in, in last singing that is. The most neat couple of stitches are in opposite coils. This makes me ashamed, in.[2]

We can imagine Mr. Arnold sputtering and fuming: "Why, that's not literature. It's perfect nonsense." There are a number of critics today who would share Mr. Arnold's conclusion. If the above paragraph was a portrait, why is it that it contains no concrete imagery that might enable the reader to relate the words to the said person? Why is punctuation used incorrectly and whimsically? What can the phrase "it shows clothes that means night gowns hours" suggest in terms of other verbal associations?

These are all questions that should be placed under a larger heading. What are the purposes of literature? We cannot speak of linguistic experimentation in literature apart from the larger purposes of the author using it. Suppose we propose that one of the purposes of literature is didactic. Historically this has certainly been one of the strongest trends in English literature. Literature can communicate a particular point or points of view by its words. The morality plays of the fifteenth century communicated to their audience ways in which they could be good Christians. The American proletarian novels of the 1930s told their audience how to be good Marxists. Whatever "message" a literature that heavily emphasizes the didactic might carry, the style is common. Words in such literature are used simply; the purpose is plainly one of semantic intelligibility and clarity. I have never heard of a political propaganda tract written impressionistically or after the fashion of the French symbolists. Even the French surrealists led by André Breton, who believed so strongly in radical linguistic experimentation, wrote their ideological platforms in the most simple and straightforward style.[3] The more an author attempts to present a coherent, concrete point of view for his readers, the more his language usages will indicate a preference for semantic clarity, a clarity usually achieved by means of conventional syntax and word choices.

On the other hand, consider the art of the French symbolist poets such as Verlaine or Mallarmé. They eschewed using language for explicit semantic communication, and saw poetic language as a mysterious music composed of new words united by a revolutionary syntax. Edmund Wilson supplies us with Paul Valéry's view of the symbolist revolution:

Literature, according to Valéry, has become "an art which is based on the abuse of language—that is, it is based on *language as a creator of illusions, and not on language as a means of transmitting realities* [my italics]. Everything which makes a language more precise, everything which emphasizes its practical character, all the changes which it undergoes in the interests of a more rapid transmission and an easier diffusion, are contrary to its function as a poetic instrument."[4]

Valéry's statement raises several issues crucial to our discussion. First of all, Valéry had the foresight to distinguish between language used in a one-to-one correspondence with ob-

jective reality and language with little or no correspondence
with reality. To the symbolists, the only true poetic language
is one with no corresponding ties to reality. The justification
for such a theory was grounded in the belief that a poem should
create an alternative reality in opposition to, or at the very least
in a creative dialogue with, social reality. This distinction is
supported by Robert Kelly in the following manner:

> For the past hundred years, there has been a . . . possibility:
> to sustain life by the creation of new forms, genuine new verbal
> structures. . . . The work of Whitman or Rimbaud in the nine-
> teenth century—with awful slowness—has at last alerted us to the
> possibility of a poem that means something. I mean a poem that
> is not, like a tune we choose to hear or neglect, *something for the
> sake of something else* [my italics] like a print tacked up on the
> wall to hide the wall. I mean a poem that means something because
> it is no longer *about* something but *is* something. . . .[5]

As Kelly notes, this movement toward "genuine new verbal structures" that create substantial realities is a modern phenomenon. Valéry's statement appears only a decade prior to
the first stories of Gertrude Stein. I entitled this book *Gertrude
Stein and the Literature of the Modern Consciousness* because
I concur with Valéry's feeling that modern literature has become the showplace for a revolutionary use of language.

Let us carry Valéry's conclusions further. If the language
of modern literature attempts to turn away from socially objective reality in order to create its own realities, what kind of
linguistic means must be used to attain its goal? Conventional
syntax and word choices have been accepted by the public as
properly corresponding to the reality they live in. If I say "I
am typing on a typewriter" I have left little doubt in most
listeners' minds as to what action I am describing. I have used
words with referents which are immediately and clearly recognized. I have organized my referents in a sequence recognizable
to most native speakers. But suppose I reorganize the sentence
to read "typewriter a on am typing I." Whatever worth (probably minuscule) this new verbal structure has as an object of

art, one thing is certain. This phrase no longer belongs to the realm of language used in socially accepted reality. It is semantically void unless we organize the words back into their original sequence, which would probably be the first response of many readers. Perhaps the problem would be handled in the following manner. The reader would call "typewriter a on am typing I" nonsense and then proceed to make sense of it by putting it into conventional syntax.

But what does our hypothetical reader mean by calling "typewriter a on am typing I" nonsense? Valéry was being extremely naïve when he distinguished symbolist language from conventional language on the grounds that "symbolist language creates illusions." All language creates illusions. The phrase "I am typing on a typewriter" is every bit as illusionary as "typewriter a on am typing I." The world of my experience cannot be simply segmented into discrete words implying the possession of identifying qualities and clearly defined verbal transactions. In an 1881 lecture entitled "Reflex Action and Theism," William James (one of Gertrude Stein's most significant instructors) said:

> We have no organ or faculty to appreciate the simply given order. The real world as it is given objectively at this moment is the sum total of all its being and events now. But can we think of such a sum. . . . While I talk and the flies buzz, a sea gull catches a fish at the mouth of the Amazon, a tree falls in the Adirondack wilderness, a man sneezes in Germany, a horse dies in Tattany and twins are born in France. What does that mean? Does the contemporaneity of these events with one another, and with a million others as disjointed, form a rational bond between them, and unite them into anything that resembles for us a world?[6]

Our syntax, our ways of combining words, is grounded in Aristotelian logic—a logic that made considerable sense at the time of its inception and makes less sense every century since. A linguistic logic based upon laws of direct causality and linear time cannot authentically correspond to a universe of possibilities such as James describes. And James's model of the world is our modern inheritance.

We are left, therefore, with the conclusion that the sole distinguishing point between "I am typing on a typewriter" and "typewriter a on am typing I" is that one is accepted by the majority of people as a "proper" correspondence phrase to describe the process of typing and that the other is reserved for lunatics, speech pathologists, and poets. The point is that we are trained and conditioned in our language learning from the earliest age to be highly conscious of grammar as a means of expressing in a "proper" way what one sees in reality. Suppose that the way we speak and write of the world determines how and what we see in it?

The American linguists Edward Sapir and Benjamin Whorf have advanced this hypothesis, and raised a considerable storm of controversy that has continued to the present day. They reason that the way we think is conditioned by the structure of the language we use to think in. Our language compels us to consider time in terms of three rigidly defined tenses. Yet our philosophy and science, our William Jameses, our Einsteins, our Bergsons, tell us that objective reality can never be considered in such divisions. The past encroaches upon the present as the present flows into the future. How can we be conscious of true time, what Bergson calls "duration," so long as we think by way of a logic chained to Aristotelian logic?

We are only conscious of time as our language allows us to be conscious of it. So let us return to literature, the symbolists, and Gertrude Stein for a moment.

If the Whorf hypothesis that we have examined is correct, then the symbolists created a new consciousness by way of a new syntax. By placing words in the most unorthodox sequences possible and by choosing words with no immediately known referents, the reader is faced with only two alternatives. Either he can brand the stuff nonsense and reorganize the words to make conventional sense, or he can consider the phrase as an artful construction in its own right. Kenneth Rexroth proposes that

Gertrude Stein did this with words. You say that poetry is different, disinterested, and structured. It is not the same kind of thing as "Please pass the butter" which is a simple imperative. But Gertrude Stein showed . . . that if you focus your attention on "Please pass the butter" and put it through enough permutations and combinations, it begins to take on a kind of glow, the splendor of which is called "aesthetic object." This is a trick of the manipulation of attention.[7]

It is not surprising to hear that Gertrude Stein began her academic career as a psychologist concerned with manipulating attention through unorthodox linguistic structures. My little experiment with the phrases about the typewriter was nothing more than a demonstration of Gertrude Stein's craft, which we will examine later in detail. The point here is that Miss Stein's syntax, like that of the symbolists before her, seeks to disturb the reader's conventional consciousness of words and their so-called corresponding realities and compels the reader to enter a realm of aesthetic possibilities and values foreign to his experience in his practical reality. To differentiate literary work such as Miss Stein's from what we earlier called the didactic or informational, I would use the term "consciousness altering." The meaning of my term is twofold.

First I refer to the ability of such literature to alter the quality, the phenomenology, of the reader's consciousness. By qualities, I refer to density (the diversity of phenomena that can exist simultaneously in the mind), continuity or discontinuity (the breaks, if any, that occur in the flow of consciousness), and speed (the duration of mental time taken for the phenomenon to pass through the reader's consciousness). If these terms seem alien to our conventional literary terms it is only because these issues of density, continuity, and speed simply did not exist in our literary language until a century ago. These terms have no meaning for literature created out of the conventional syntax. Under the old rules density or consciousness was no problem because phenomena were parceled out in neat bundles of discrete orders of nouns and verbs. Con-

tinuity was no problem since the old grammatical rules for
properly organizing sentences were accepted and discontinuities simply had no place in the old aesthetics. Speed of consciousness was unthought of since the reading time, left to
right, of any sentence was assumed to be the mental time taken
for its comprehension. With the creation of a radically new
syntax, these categories of density, continuity, and speed become crucial to our understanding.

Consider a second meaning of the phrase "consciousness
altering" literature. In addition to altering the quality of consciousness such writing alters the quantity—the size—of the
field of consciousness. I use the phrase "consciousness expan-
sion" with caution, since it is presently linked in the public
mind with drug experimentation. However, this is exactly
what such literature proposes to do. It is more than a coinci-
dence that William S. Burroughs, the leading American novelist of the drug experience, studied Gertrude Stein's method as
a student at Harvard.

I am therefore proposing that we consider a range of Gertrude Stein's writing in the light of the concepts I have out-
lined in this introduction. I am *not* suggesting that we consider
Miss Stein's literary *oeuvre* entirely in these terms. Although
I feel the main thrust of her work centers on this issue of language and consciousness, I am in no way neglecting the purely
literary and, most importantly, purely human concerns of her
work.

One reason I am drawn to Gertrude Stein's work is the
skill with which she wears the masks of both poet and psychologist. I see her works as demonstrations, perhaps the most developed demonstrations of our age, of the consciousness and
language problem. But what gives her art the human interest
it holds is the fact that her psychological laboratory is the
world of human personality. The Negro woman Melanctha in
Three Lives, the generations of German immigrant stock in
The Making of Americans, the Saints of *Four Saints in Three
Acts*, Mrs. Reynolds of the novel of the same name—these are

the characters through which her theories speak and develop. And while their words herald the development of a new syntax they also carry the emotional charge of real people in real situations. Unlike the symbolists, Gertrude Stein felt eminently at home in the world and her work, however "other-worldly" in construct, shows a sympathetic understanding with "things as they are."

One further warning should be sounded before we proceed. This book deals with a variety of issues in linguistics and psychology that have not as yet been, and may never be, finally proved. The areas of psycholinguistics discussed here are still largely uncharted territories. What Edmund Wilson wrote in *Axel's Castle* four decades ago holds equally true today:

As I have pointed out in connection with Gertrude Stein, our ideas about the "logic" of language are likely to be superficial. The relation of words to what they convey—that is, to the processes behind them and the processes to which they give rise in those who listen to or read them—is still a very mysterious one.[8]

My purpose is to present possible systems through which Miss Stein's work can be elucidated. Speech pathology, psycholinguistics, structural linguistics, and linguistic anthropology may not provide us with any final answers to the dilemmas raised by Miss Stein's work. They may, indeed, create more questions that will have to remain unanswered.

But I contend that this is the proper approach to a woman who asked, in her final words spoken from a hospital bed, "What is the answer?" Then smiled and said: "On the other hand, what is the question?"

II
"Melanctha":
Toward a Definition
of Character

I began to get enormously interested in hearing how everybody said the same thing over and over again with infinite variations but over and over again until finally if you listened with great intensity you could hear it rise and fall and tell all that there was inside them, not so much by the actual words they said or the thoughts they had but the movement of their thoughts and words endlessly the same and endlessly different.[1]

—Gertrude Stein

Gertrude Stein's first published works were psychological experiments conducted at Radcliffe with the assistance of Leon Solomons. The experiments focused on normal and induced motor automatism—actions located on the threshold between consciousness and unconsciousness. Automatic writing and reading were the phenomena examined. The results of these experiments were published in the *Harvard Psychological Review*. Fortunately they are also available in vastly simplified form in Gertrude Stein's *Lectures in America*.

What makes a minute examination of these experiments difficult for the layman is the fact that they reflect the concerns of the science of psychology circa 1900. One factor we must keep in mind is that for Gertrude Stein psychology meant the psychology of William James and his followers. In the first decade of this century the work of Freud and Jung was virtually unheard of. The problems that psychology examined—What is consciousness? How does consciousness relate to the whole personality? Is consciousness continuous or discontinuous? What is the meaning of automatic functioning? How does unconscious knowledge pass into consciousness?— grew out of James's massive *Principles of Psychology*.

Certain assumptions that James makes concerning the human personality deserve to be stated if for no other reason than that they are also Gertrude Stein's assumptions. Foremost among these is the Jamesian assumption of the universe as pluralistic. The world was seen as teeming with possibilities, any of which could be actualized if man chose to do so. For James, a man's personality is the product of what he most emphasizes in his field of consciousness. Out of the thousands of sense impressions a man receives at any waking moment of his life, only a few are selected and even fewer are attended to. A college lecturer on Spinoza cannot afford to entertain thoughts of pheasant for long in his classroom, nor can a chef consider Spinoza to the fullest in his kitchen. The personality estab-

lishes and rigidifies his choice of objects of attention by means
of *habit*.

> Habit is thus the enormous fly-wheel of society, its most pre-
> cious conservative agent. It alone is what keeps us all within the
> bounds of ordinance, and saves the children of fortune from the
> envious uprising of the poor. . . . It dooms us all to fight out
> the battle of life upon the lines of our nature or our early choice and
> to make the best of a pursuit that disagrees, because there is no
> other for which we are fitted. . . .[2]

At the risk of oversimplifying James, there is a strong
tinge of determinism and even characterology in the paragraph
above. The phrase "fight out the battle of life upon the lines
of our nature" brings to mind Lamarck, Darwin, and Fichte,
but certainly does not recall any twentieth-century philosopher of radical individualism. It also strikes me as a curiously
un-American statement in temperament. As R. W. B. Lewis[3]
indicates in his study of character in American literature,
America traditionally has been the home of the new Adam:
the man innocent until proved guilty. The Calvinistic fires of
wrath that judge infants as saved or damned at birth have been
all but extinguished in this century. Lewis argues that it is a
characteristic of the American character to think of the human personality as a tabula rasa: a man is nothing more than
the sum total of his experiences. The radical individualism of
Thoreau and Whitman carries this premise to its logical conclusion. If a man is the total of what he lives, a man may
choose to radically alter his personality by radically altering
his life style. This belief assumes an extreme plasticity of character, a belief many of us take for granted. Certainly the
phrase common to the American frontiersman—"going West
to start a new life"—is alien to the European temperament. In
America one can move and seemingly begin one's life over
again. In Europe one's life is one's life: a struggle within the
boundaries of personality.

I am insisting on this distinction because it is a crucial idea
in Gertrude Stein's personality theory. She is one of the very

few American writers of our time who reject the Lockean model of a limitless plasticity of character. She follows James in seeing the personality in terms of a fixed nature, a central "core," subject to alteration by experience, but only subject to change within the limitation imposed by the entire character structure.

But even more than her mentor James, Gertrude Stein accepts the idea of characterology. A characterology implies that all persons can be classified into categories of psychological types. Again, we must consider such an idea in the light of nineteenth-century psychology. Early psychology was involved in a desperate struggle with the physical sciences in order to establish its own legitimacy as a science. All the other sciences had developed broad structural frames within which their observations could be categorized. As simple-minded as a characterology appears to us circa 1970, it held significance to the psychologist of 1900. As Miss Stein comments in her lectures:

> Then as I say I became more interested in psychology, and one of the things I did was testing reactions of the average college student in a state of normal activity and in a state of fatigue induced by their examinations. I was supposed to be interested in their reactions but soon I found that I was not but instead that I was enormously interested in the types of characters . . .[4]

An acceptance of characterology brings with it a host of complementary assumptions. First, it implies that those elements most central to the character structure vary little if at all during the person's lifetime. Secondly, it underplays the significance of experience in shaping character. Donald Sutherland in his *Gertrude Stein: A Biography of Her Work* provides this summary of Miss Stein's characterology:

> Within the single individual the diffusion or concentration, the gentleness or toughness, the ways of attack or defense or dependency . . . do not essentially vary. In short the whole composition of the character can really be present in any moment, in

the continuous present, and not as a thing remembered, not as an accumulation of personal history.[5]

Let us begin to consider the consequences of such a personality theory when the theory becomes used artistically in a work of literature. The portrayal of character in twentieth-century fiction is often accomplished through the character's "stream of consciousness." In Joyce, in Proust, in Virginia Woolf, the character's consciousness is an invaluable repository of past experience that encroaches upon the present. In *Swann's Way* it is the sight of madeleines that open the Pandora's box of Swann's youth and sends physic vibrations racing into the present moment. The stream-of-consciousness novelist must believe in the radical malleability of personality or else the very term "consciousness stream" would be rendered meaningless. For Proust and company the character is wherever the consciousness stream carries him. Hence the importance of the "epiphany," the sudden, unvolitional consciousness breakthrough as a prime determinant of character change. The stream-of-consciousness character is a product of all his past experiences carried into the present. Thus it is not without significance that the stream-of-consciousness novel developed in the same decades as Freudian and Jungian psychoanalysis. Both Freud and Jung anticipated the stream-of-consciousness technique by imploring their patients to free-associate until a key to the present direction of the consciousness stream could be found.

Where does Gertrude Stein stand in relation to this dominant trend in twentieth-century literature?

In absolute, unwavering opposition to it.

Once she accepted a characterology the possibility of any major character changes, whether through epiphany or willed action, was unlikely. Sutherland offers this explanation:

If the character does not change, if its interior and exterior history has no important influence on it, and if it is the definition and description of types of characters that interest the writer, the problem is one of projecting character in time without a sequence of events and all the context of irrelevant accidents. This leads naturally to repetition, the constantly new assertion and realization of the same simple thing, an existence with its typical qualities, not an event.[6]

It is within this light that I suggest we consider "Melanctha," the most accomplished of the three tales in *Three Lives*.

In beginning writing I wrote a book called *Three Lives* this was written in 1905. I wrote a negro story called *Melanctha*. In that there was a constant recurring and beginning there was a marked direction in the direction of being in the present although naturally I had been accustomed to past present and future, and why, because the composition formation around me was a prolonged present.[7]

All of the three lives depicted in *Three Lives* describe simple personalities in conflict with a complex, demanding, interpersonal situation. "The Good Anna" portrays the fate of a simple, honest, utterly straightforward German servant woman subject to the impositions of unstraightforward employers and friends. "The Gentle Lena" follows a similar schema, though extreme naïveté and frailty have been added to the protagonist's personality.

I consider "Melanctha" of the greatest human and artistic importance because of the unrelentless depiction of the human personality falling in and out of love. The Anna and Lena stories approach the level of Flaubert's fable, "A Simple Soul," in their insistence on depicting only the surface psychology of the main character.

Gertrude Stein notes in *The Autobiography of Alice B. Toklas* that the two precipitating events that led to the writing of *Three Lives* were the translation of Flaubert's *Three Fables* and the purchase of a Cézanne portrait.[8] The connections between Flaubert's fables and those of Miss Stein have been admirably described by Donald Sutherland. There is only one point I wish to add to Mr. Sutherland's analysis. The "primitive" or "rough hewn" quality of Flaubert's characters comes from the limited perspective the author affords us of the character. Flaubert's "Simple Soul" is utterly simple-minded, single-minded, one-dimensional. Hence she is a personage in a fable. We do not read fables to discover the innermost psychological workings of the character. The character's significance is revealed in action—those few actions which bring the quintessential features of the personality into play, into the open for the reader's examination. In Flaubert's *Three Fables* his characters never say more about themselves than they know— and they know very little. As a reader you must come to grips with each character's own limited vision, temporally, spatially, psychologically. This facet of Flaubert applied perfectly to Stein.

Although what we said above about Flaubert has application to all *Three Lives*, it seems to hold the least relevance when we consider Melanctha. Whatever else she is Melanctha is not a fable character. She is psychologically intricate. She is strangely both one-dimensional and multidimensional, as we will presently examine. She is, Gertrude Stein informs us, "subtle, intelligent, half white"; "full with mystery and subtle movements and denials and vague distrusts and complicated disillusions"; "pale yellow and mysterious and a little pleasant"; "had a break neck courage and a tongue that could be very nasty."

You have just read all the important information about Melanctha that Gertrude Stein gives in one hundred and twenty pages of narrative. Ask yourself the question Who is Melanctha? and, unless you are satisfied with the rather trite adjectival clusters listed above, you will have no answer.

Is the character revealed in her action? Melanctha does absolutely nothing in one hundred pages but attend to her sick mother and overdemanding friends, chase three men, and fall in love with one. She falls out of love. She later dies of tuberculosis. End of story.

Is the story's worth established by its style? Melanctha is revealed by an omniscient narrator and by her own conversations. The narrator sounds like an idiot, endlessly repeating

Melanctha's salient traits ("subtle, half white," etc., etc.) and provides an absolute minimum of relevant personal data. Melanctha's own speech patterns are asyntactic, highly monotonous, and often dull.

Why is "Melanctha" considered Gertrude Stein's finest achievement by even her most demanding critics?

"Melanctha" reveals the consciousness alterations of a simple character by means unique in modern literature.

In "Melanctha," Gertrude Stein's characterology and theory of personality come to life. Her composition coordinates the movements of consciousness with the narrative flow in a variety of ways. Among these are *active author intervention in the narrative flow*.

"Melanctha" opens with the sentence:

> Rose Johnson made it very hard to bring her baby to its birth.
> Melanctha Herbert who was Rose Johnson's friend, did everything any woman could.[9]

Some hundred pages later this item is reiterated in almost the same fashion. Melanctha's friendship with Rose occurs toward the end of Melanctha's life chronologically, yet we are introduced to Melanctha through this incident. We are also informed in the first paragraph that Rose's baby will die, that Melanctha attended Rose both before and after her pregnancy. But after the sentence "Here the baby was born, and here it died, and then Rose went back to her house again with Sam," neither Rose nor Sam are mentioned again until the very end of the narrative. With no other transitional bridge than a new paragraph Miss Stein moves from Rose to the time of Melanctha's adolescence, long before she met Rose.

The discontinuities in narrative time are quite intentional. First, by giving the reader significant character information out of linear sequence the reader is forced to weigh all incoming information *equally*.

Consider for a moment the development of a villain's character in a murder mystery. The reader looks for clues re-

vealing the villain's character in each chapter; he totals them
so that by the tale's climax the clues add up to the "solution."
"Of course *x* was the murderer," we say, "because in Chapter
One he did this, later he did that . . . ," etc. If the vast simplification can be forgiven, all of us read novels by "totaling the
clues given." If the average man on the street prefers Mickey
Spillane to James Joyce it might be because Joyce's temporal
schema presupposes an enormously sophisticated and discrimi-
nating reader who is willing to process the raw data as given
unsequentially by the author.

But Gertrude Stein's use of unsequential narrative time in
"Melanctha" is initially even more baffling than Joyce's. The
broken time flow in *Ulysses* is justified by the fact that any
character's stream-of-consciousness statements have roots somewhere in past experience. By contrast all the action in "Melanctha" takes place in what Gertrude Stein calls the "continuous present." The illusion of eternal presentness is supported by a number of stylistic devices—the most obvious
being Miss Stein's use of present participles. This is most
acutely revealed in the central passages of the story: the lovers'
dialogue between Melanctha and Jeff Campbell. Jeff speaks:

> . . . I certainly do believe strong in *loving,* and in *being* good
> to everybody, and *trying* to understand what they all need, to help
> them. . . . I am always so busy with my *thinking* about my work
> I am *doing* and so I don't have time for just *fooling.* . . . [my
> italics].[10]

Let us consider this passage in terms of the entire narrative. The most significant event in the story is Melanctha's
falling in and out of love with Jeff. I emphasize falling in and
out because the story is concerned with the process of coming
to terms with passion. Melanctha and Jeff observed in the light
of a characterology are polar opposites. Where Jeff is cautious
to the point of timidity, Melanctha is adventurous to the point
of recklessness. Where Jeff realizes depth and intensity with
slowness, Melanctha reacts with lightening speed. Melanctha

and Jeff can never marry because of the conflicting speeds of
their personalities. Gertrude Stein's genius is revealed in the
way in which she records the speed differences in the speech
patterns of her characters. Jeff's speech is loaded with participles, qualifying adjectives, qualifying clauses. All indicate the
slowness of his consciousness flow. Jeff "believes" in loving, he
doesn't love. He "tries" to understand. There is the continuous
approaching of passionate self-definition, never the actual en-
gagement of being in passion. Jeff's "approachings" occur in
the continuous present because at every moment of the narrative Jeff Campbell is essentially the same person. Jeff continually reasserts who he is by how he speaks, as does
Melanctha:

> Yes *I certainly do understand* you when you talk so Dr.
> Campbell. *I certainly do understand* now what you mean by what
> you was always saying to me. *I certainly do understand* Dr.
> Campbell that you mean you don't believe it's right to love any-
> body [my italics].[11]

As Jeff's consciousness is stuffed with precautionary
words, Melanctha is supported by unqualified assertions ("I
certainly do" is an often repeated refrain.) While Jeff's patterns show a slow, ruminative consideration of information,
Melanctha's reveal an impulsive, immediate response to data.
The differing speeds of consciousness stand in bold relief since
only these two minds are considered in most of the narrative.
The discontinuities in narrative time serve to emphasize the
two different consciousness flows. We are introduced to Melanctha at a time late in her life, after her relations with Jeff
have terminated. We are then carried through time up to her
relationship, and again carried back to where we began. The
discontinuous narrative is preferred over the linear narrative because Melanctha is the same person throughout. The incidents
at the beginning of her life are no more significant in molding
her character than the incidents at any other point in her life.
The character is always in the present because for Gertrude

Stein the present is "the twentieth-century moment of composition." For a character to live for the reader, the character must always be who she is, must always be *being*. And being implies the continual reassertion of what is through all its slight permutations, a process that Miss Stein links with motion pictures:

> Funnily enough the cinema has offered a solution of this thing. By a continuously moving picture of any one there is no memory of any other thing and there is that thing existing. . . .[12]

The analogy to motion pictures leads us to Gertrude Stein's second device to reveal the differences in consciousness flow—*graduated degrees of syntactic displacement*.

> "Melanctha Herbert," began Jeff Campbell, "I certainly after all this time I know you, I certainly do, know little, real about you. You see, Melanctha, it's like this way, with me. . . . You see it's just this way, with me, now, Melanctha. Sometimes you seem like one kind of a girl to me, and sometimes you are like a girl that is all different to me, and the two kinds of girls is certainly very different to each other. . . ."[13]

Sentences are repeated with the slightest alterations. Compare: "You see, Melanctha, it's like this way with me" with "You see it's just this way, with me, now." The sentence structure is changed ever so slightly by commas. Commas are inserted not for syntactic correctness but for rhythmic, tonal emphasis. The same words are put into a different sequence in order to emphasize the recurring sameness and the recurring difference of the thought. These changes are graduated. By graduated I imply that the changes increase in number and complexity in direct relation to the emotion to be conveyed. It is when Jeff is most passionately engaged in trying to win Melanctha's love that the permutations between sentences are most complex.

It is because of these graduated, minute syntactic changes that Gertrude Stein's prose can be called "cubistic." Much as Duchamp in the "Nude Descending a Staircase" creates the il-

lusion of a figure in continuous motion by drawing repetitious
lines of supposed motion around the body of the still figure, so
Stein gives the illusion of a figure with a continuous present
reality by permutating his speech patterns. These permutations
make Jeff's consciousness appear continuous while it is actually extremely discontinuous.

"And then, Melanctha, sometimes you certainly do seem sort
of cruel, and not to care about people being hurt or in trouble,
something so hard about you it makes me sometimes real nervous,
sometimes somehow like you always, like your being, with 'Mis'
Herbert. You sure did everything that any woman could, Melanctha, I certainly never did see anybody do things any better. . . ."[14]

There is no logically sequential stream of thought here
that can be diagrammed—A leads to B leads to C. We are presented with a discontinuous fabric of observations and feelings
and judgments that appear unified and continuous because of
the repetitive grammatical patterns. Let us reconsider a quotation from Gertrude Stein's *Lectures in America* that we mentioned earlier:

I began to get enormously interested in hearing how everybody said the same thing over and over with infinite variations.
. . . If you listened with great intensity you could hear it rise and
fall . . . *not so much by the actual words they said* . . . but by
the movement of their thought and words.[15]

The consciousness flow as revealed through language has
three qualities. The first we considered was speed: the duration of time it takes for phenomena to pass in and out of consciousness. We indicated earlier how Melanctha and Jeff's
characters could never become synchronized and how their
discrepancy in consciousness speed was indicated by their
speech patterns. The second quality of the consciousness flow is
continuity, and we have indicated how Jeff's patterns give the
illusion of continuity while being in reality discontinuous,
dissociated fragments. I would suggest that a relation can be

drawn here between consciousness speed and consciousness continuity. The objects in one's perceptual field can be fragmented by either accelerating or decelerating mental time. If I accelerate the consciousness flow, as a drug like lysergic acid might cause me to do, my desk, my typewriter, my books melt into one another, merge, de-substantiate; if I decelerate my consciousness flow, as a hypnotic trance might cause me to do, another variety of discontinuity will occur.

Beginning with "Melanctha" and continuing throughout her entire writing career, Gertrude Stein explores the possibility of decelerating mental time. "Melanctha" represents the first step in a lifelong series of experiments to discover the relationship between decelerated time consciousness and its correlative in language, particularly in syntactic patterns.

The third quality of the conscious flow revealed in the Melanctha speech patterns is density. By density I imply the number of mental events that can be simultaneously held in the consciousness. For example:

Jeff always loved to watch everything as it was growing, and he loved all the colors in the trees and on the ground, and the little, new, bright colored bugs he found in the moist ground and in the grass he loved to lie on and in which he was so busy searching.[16]

Six discrete events—evocations of a scene involving verbal action—are linked only by the word "and." (1. Jeff always loved to watch everything. . . . 2. Jeff always loved to watch everything as it was growing. . . . 3. . . . he loved all the colors. . . . 4. . . . bugs he found in the ground. . . . 5. . . . in the grass he loved to lie on. . . . 6. . . . he was so busy searching. . . .) Number 4 implies direct verbal action that is an event although the event is evoked indirectly. The catalogue creates the illusion of six events occurring *simultaneously* in one present moment and so creates the effect of *maximal density* of consciousness. As speed and continuity are related, so are density and continuity. A sentence like the pas-

sage quoted above with its concentration of events syntactically linked gives the illusion of continuity although the events
described did not in actuality all occur in the same moment of
time and have no logical reason to be strung together.

When Gertrude Stein spoke of listening to the *movement*
of words rather than merely what the words said, it might
be because she was concerned with the *quality* of character consciousness as opposed to the contents of character
consciousness.

How does the consciousness of Melanctha move?

By moving in discontinuous time, by endlessly graduated
permutations, by concentrated sentences of verbal and purely
descriptive action. The words are less important for their ideational, semantic weight than for their relation to all the other
words in the speech stream. The peculiar character consciousness emerges in a peculiar syntax, a personal grammar specifically suited for the speed, continuity, and density of the characters to be observed.

In "Melanctha" we see how Gertrude Stein's genius found
in the American Negro's natural speech patterns the seeds for
her peculiar word organizations. While the dialogues maintain
a remarkable fidelity to the actual Negro speech Gertrude
Stein heard around her while working in the Negro areas of
Baltimore[17] as a medical aide, the dialogue also stands as an au-
thentic aesthetic construct, an accomplished experiment in cubistic prose art.

"Melanctha" and indeed, the whole of *Three Lives* have
their roots in Dreiserian naturalism since the book's language
is rooted in the speech of the tribe, however subtly altered by
Miss Stein to suit her own ends. The works that follow depend
less on permutating the language as heard in daily discourse
and represent a motion outward from realism to abstractionism.

"Melanctha" has its roots in the actual life of the American Negro and although the Negro characters seem to exist in
a vague or nonexistent landscape, they still emerge in "Melanctha" as real persons; Melanctha, Jeff Campbell, Rose, and Sam
are revealed in the movements of their words, their peculiar

turns of phrases, pauses, coloristic adjectives, or declarative verbs. For Gertrude Stein the discovery of character depends upon the most intense hearing of what the character has to say. And so "Melanctha" is fascinating in what it does not attend to as a work of art.

The plot is simplistic, the characters common, the rhetoric clubfooted. The local environmental color of Negro life is entirely neglected. The actual physical descriptions of the characters are unsatisfying. Love is described without sexual description, selfishness is depicted without concrete example. Neither Melanctha nor Jeff are the better for having fallen in love, and the story ends the same way it began.

The miracle is that "Melanctha" succeeds despite ignoring all these facets of the conventional narrative. It succeeds by giving the reader an uncanny feeling for the peculiar qualities of mind of these two characters with their most common words.

Three Lives succeeds by offering an alternative vision of life in the most simple yet moving terms: the words central to being.

III
The Making
of Americans:
The Narrative
Redefined

In faith Euphues thou hast told me a long tale, the beginning I have forgotten the middle I understand not and the end hangeth not together. In the meanwhile it were best for me to take a nap for I cannot brook these seas which provoke my stomache sore.

—from the *Complete Works of John Lyly,*
the quotation found in Gertrude Stein's notebooks
for *The Making of Americans*[1]

Three Lives marked a radical turning point in Gertrude Stein's artistic career. Although the book's circulation was limited it came into the hands of readers as distinguished as Edmund Wilson, Eugene O'Neill, and Ford Maddox Ford. The response from fellow writers and literary critics was generally positive. Even those critics most hostile to Miss Stein's pursuits acknowledge *Three Lives* as her masterpiece. In spite of its stylistic eccentricities, *Three Lives* has a broadly based appeal because of the subject matter of the stories themselves. Richard Wright tells of reading "Melanctha" aloud to a group of illiterate Negro workmen during their lunch hour and reports their delight in hearing incidents descibed in words central to their daily living experience. *Three Lives* represents the last of Gertrude Stein's work to be firmly rooted in Dreiserian naturalism or realism. *The Making of Americans* and all the major prose works that follow refer to objective, external reality as a secondary, fragmentary phenomenon of lesser consequence than subjective, mental reality.

So *The Making of Americans* represents an attempt to create for the reader an aesthetic reality, substantial within itself, with an absolute minimum of references to the objective world. This hardly seems remarkable in itself. Certainly most mythological and fantasy literature shares a similar outlook. But what makes Gertrude Stein's book revolutionary is that it is the narrative of an actual family's progress in America over a span of generations. The subject matter is mundane, commonplace, middle-class, and frankly banal. Consider for a moment the task of writing a family chronicle with the following conditions imposed upon you as author: you must not put the family members in any definite temporal or spatial context; you must not maintain a sequential, logical time sequence of events; you must not consider any one event a family character experiences in his lifetime any more significant than any other event experienced by any other relative at any time. As well as these negative impositions, consider these positive injunctions: you must enumerate in your family chronicle every single person ever to come in contact with the household. You must record the lives of the family members from birth to death in all cases. You must clearly show the changes of mind that occur through the passages of generations as reflected in politics, art, sex, life style, religion, morality, and economics.

The conditions listed above are a summary of Gertrude Stein's concerns in *The Making of Americans*. The reasons behind these principles and their implications in this narrative we will now consider.

The Making of Americans is the "history" of two families: the Dehnings and the Herslands. Both families are traced back to their middle-class roots in Europe. I have put "history" in quotation marks because *The Making of Americans* is anything but family history as we are accustomed to view it in other literatures. In a novel that traces a family history through generations—Thomas Mann's *Buddenbrooks*, for instance—every effort is maintained by the author to literally trace the characteristics of the most contemporary generation discussed back to its ancestors. Phylogeny recapitulates ontogeny, and so we read through hundreds of pages of Mann's narrative writing until in the final chapters we are rewarded; all the seemingly irrelevant details of the family chronicle fall into a coherent pattern by the time the book's climax is reached.

Surely one of the pleasures of reading Proust's *Remembrance of Things Past* in its entirety is the sense of final cohesion that brings together the enormous weight of detail with which Proust so liberally decorates his narrative.

By contrast, one of the severe difficulties of even reading *The Making of Americans* in its entirety is the narrative discontinuities in a book that purports to be a "family history." For example the book opens with Gertrude Stein's reworking of a quote from Aristotle's ethics:

Once an angry man dragged his father along the ground through his own orchard. "Stop!" cried the groaning old man at last, "Stop! I did not drag my father beyond this tree."

It is hard living down the tempers we are born with. We all begin well, for in our youth there is nothing we are more intolerant of than our own sins writ large in others and we fight them fiercely in ourselves; but we grow old and we see that these sins our sins are of all sins the really harmless ones to own, nay that they give charm to any character. . . .[2]

This is Gertrude Stein speaking. And it is Gertrude Stein's omnipresent voice as narrator that resounds through the half million words of narrative. From the very start there is no ambiguity as to the nature of the narrator. She is perfectly in control of the thematic flow at all times. She is repetitious, for our particular storyteller is also a theorizing psychologist who believes the essence of the human personality is revealed in repetition:

Repeating then is in every one, in every one their being and their feeling and their way of realizing everything and every one of them comes out in repeating. More and more then every one comes to be clear to some one.[3]

But the most striking characteristic of our narrator is her astonishing verbosity. Nearly a thousand pages of closely packed prose and a half million words are employed to depict the progress of the Dehning and Hersland families. Why this prolixity? Is the verbosity an outgrowth of the author's attempt to write the complete family chronicle of these families with every detail clear and intact?

Let us return to the plot of *The Making of Americans* a moment. After her prefacing paragraph stating the major didactic thread of the book (it is hard living down the tempers we are born with, etc.) Miss Stein proceeds to discuss the phenomena of being an American, a parent, a grandparent, a child. Not until the seventh page of the book is a specific family member, Henry Dehning, mentioned. Here is our introduction to him:

Henry Dehning was a grown man and for his day a rich one when his father died away and left them. Truly he had made everything for himself very different; but it is not as a young man making himself rich that we are now to feel him, he is for us an old grown man telling it all over to his children.[4]

We are told by the author "it is not as a young man that we are now to feel him." We receive the impression of the narrator as a master puppeteer controlling all the puppet's strings. This sense of narrator dominance is reinforced by the length of time that passes before a single, concrete personage is mentioned. This technique of cataloguing all the general human possibilities and then zooming in upon one specific family character occurs throughout the text. Consider this description prior to the introduction of Marsha Hersland:

There are many that I know and I know it. They are many that I know and they know it. They are all of them themselves and they repeat it and I hear it. Always I listen to it. . . . They repeat themselves now and I listen to it. Every way that they do it now I hear it.[5]

I am insisting on this point because *The Making of Americans* gives the illusion of being a family history by opposing a few well-defined character descriptions against an illusionary backdrop of all those that have ever lived, are living, or will live. If we remember Miss Stein's notion of characterology the claim of all-inclusiveness appears less fantastic than at first sight.

Only a handful of characters from the Dehning and Hersland families are extensively described. Most of the attention is focused upon Julia Dehning, the oldest daughter of Henry Dehning, and on Alfred Hersland, the second of the three children of David Hersland. It could be argued that Julia and Alfred are the only characters in the book that emerge and are as successful artistically as the characters in *Three Lives*. The hundreds of other characters appear for brief moments, as their lives fleetingly come in contact with Julia and Alfred, and then

disappear again. When a character has "spoken his part" he re-
turns to that swelling, amorphous mass of "everyone" and
"some ones" and "all those who are living ones" and "all those
who are dead ones" that comprises the backdrop for the characters of the two families and their significant actions.

But if the central pivotal event of the book is the falling
out of love of Julia Dehning and Alfred Hersland, why must
we suffer through a thousand-page record of everyone and
everything that occurred to them during their lives? Why
must we be introduced to a regular who's who of nonentities
in the form of Mary Waxworthing, the seamstress to the Hersland family, the two governesses before Madeline Wyman,
and a host of others.

Gertrude Stein gives the raison d'être for such a technique
in the lecture "Composition as Explanation."

There is singularly nothing that makes a difference a difference in beginning and in the middle and in ending except that each
generation has something different at which they are all looking.
. . . There was [in making] a groping for using everything and
there was a groping for a continuous present and there was an
evitable beginning of beginning again and again.[6]

All of these ideas become translated into the following paragraph in *The Making of Americans*:

Sometime there is a history of each one, of every one who
ever has living in them and repeating in them and has their being
coming out from them in their repeating that is always in all being.
Sometime there is a history of everyone.[7]

The Making of Americans can be considered a "history
of everyone who ever lived, is living and will live" because for
Gertrude Stein all persons can be fitted into her characterology. The roots for her characterology are found in *Three
Lives*. Melanctha Herbert and Doctor Campbell were unable
to love because of an essential discrepancy in the rhythm, the
speed of their personalities. The same is true of Julia and Al-

fred, but in *The Making of Americans* the attempt is made to trace the roots of their discord all the way back—three generations back to European soil. The title "making of Americans" is meant to be taken literally. From the immigration of grandparents to the youngest American in the book, David Hersland, Jr., the aim is to show how the *American* consciousness is forged through the passage of generations. Such an encyclopedic task would be absurd from the start unless we grant some common pool of personality characteristics that exist as a constant from generation to generation. For Miss Stein these are the principles of the independent dependent and dependent independent personalities:

> There are always some then of the many millions of this first kind of them the independent dependent kind of them who never have it in them to have any such attacking in them. . . . Some of them have this in them as gentle pretty young innocence inside them. . . . In the second kind of them the dependent independent kind of them who have too all through their living servant girl nature in them, in this kind of them there are many there are many of them who have a scared timid submission in them with a resisting sometime somewhere in them. . . .[8]

Although the distinction between the two types always remains somehow vague, the following attributes can be classed under the two headings:

Independent Dependent:	*Dependent Independent:*
aggressive	meek
active	withdrawn, passive
independent in judgment	weak in judgment
buoyant, boisterous	shy, quiet
selfishness that can lead to sadism	selfishness that can lead to masochism, martyrdom
reckless	cautious

The left column totaled gives us a summary of Julia Dehning. The right column, of Alfred Hersland. And every single character in the book represents some combinations of elements in

either the left- or right-hand columns. It is what is most heavily
emphasized in each grouping that finally determines how a
character will live his life. It sounds like Ben Jonson's old theory of "humors" revised by a student of Jamesian psychology.
James insisted that the personality is a product of what one
chooses to pay attention to in the consciousness stream. Gertrude Stein gives the objects in the consciousness field a
weight, a quantifiable mass, and identifies the psychic self itself
as a mixture of masses. She speaks of each character as having
a "bottom nature" or psychological core and writes:

> There are some men and women having in them very much
> weakness as the bottom in them and *watery anxious feeling* and
> sometimes nervous anxious feeling in them and sometimes stubborn
> feeling in them. There are some that have *vague or vacant feeling
> in them* . . . [my italics].[9]

Passions are quantified like Elizabethan humors, and what comprises a character is his peculiar balance at any point in time.

So what changes from generation to generation is not the
type of psychological phenomenon but the distribution. What
changes is not the fact that men perceive reality but what they
choose to single out in their perception of reality. So we are
dealing with a highly peculiar variety of family history in *The
Making of Americans.* We are concerned with the gradualness
of a change in viewing the objects of consciousness through a
family's history. This sense of graduated consciousness change
between generations is dramatized by certain central incidents.

In the weeks before her marriage to Alfred Julia Dehning
shops for furniture and decorations for her new home. The
differences between generations are dramatized in the descriptions of the objects in Julia's home:

> Julia Dehning's new house was in arrangement a small edition
> of her mother's. In ways to wash, to help out all the special doctors
> in their work, in sponges, brushes, running water everywhere, in
> hygenic ways to air things and keep one's self clean and everything
> all clean, this house that Julia was to make fit for her new life

which was to come, in this it was very much like the old one she had lived in, but always here there were more plunges, douches, showers, ways to get cold water. . . . In her mother's house there were many ways to get clean but mostly they suggested cold water and a certain comfort, here in the new house was a sterner feeling, it must be a cold world, that one could keep one's soul high and clean in.[10]

Much as the illusion of describing all human beings is maintained by mentioning lists of all those servants the family ever came in contact with, so the illusion of an all-encompassing objective reality is maintained by lists of objects. Both of these "illusions" support the idea of the book as a devastatingly complete family history. Yet the entire family history is disembodied, and remains outside any definite spatial or temporal context. We know that time has passed between the marriage of Julia's mother and Julia's own marriage by the changing ideas of interior decorating. No dates are used to locate the action historically. Only two place names are mentioned, Bridgeport on the East coast and Gossols on the West. Although some critics have suggested that Bridgeport is Baltimore and Gossols is Oakland, California (assuming that Miss Stein was referring to her own childhood and adolescence spent in both cities) there is no way to prove the contention. This lack of location is fitting for a family chronicler with Gertrude Stein's biases. If the character is a mixture of tendencies determined chiefly by genealogies, the actual physical environment plays a minimal role in the molding of personality. When the few sustained descriptions of landscape occur they seem to be placed in the narrative for decorative rather than for locational purposes:

The home the rich and self made merchant makes to hold his family and himself is always like the city where his fortune has been made. In London it is like that rich and endless dark and gloomy place, in Paris it is filled with pleasant toys, cheery and light and made of gilded decoration and white paint, and in Bridgeport it was neither gloomy nor joyous but like a large and splendid canvas completely painted over but painted full of empty space.[11]

This childlikeness, the naïveté characteristic of the narrator, embodies a literal characteristic of child perception: the spatial and temporal limits are vaguely defined, if defined at all. This lack of context resembles "a large and splendid canvas completely painted over but painted full of empty space." *The Making of Americans* has more in common with a mythological family history or fable based on a family line than with a novel spanning generations such as *Buddenbrooks*. Because of an undefined, unrooted, objective setting, the characters can loom in the narrative as either giants or pygmies. Because Henry Dehning exists *in vacuo* and not in simultaneous intercourse with other fathers, he becomes *the* father figure to Julia and to the reader. When he speaks he thunders:

No I say I don't think you children will ever be good for something. No you won't ever know how to make a living, not if all the ways I have seen men make a success in working is any kind of use to tell from. Well, what do you know with all your always talking, what do you know about how good hard work is done now?[12]

And yet this man who looms so largely in Julia's life before marriage is never mentioned again except as "a dead one" after Julia's marriage. This is why a list of the importance of characters in hierarchical order is impossible. In his way Henry Dehning, who occupies about two dozen pages of text, is just as important to the family history as David Hersland, who occupies the last 250 pages of text. This is also why every character, whether seamstress or governess, ever to come into direct contact with the Hersland or Dehning families is just as important to the chronicle as any brother or sister. If in any given moment of living we are what we attend to in our consciousness field, then a seamstress takes on the same weight as a queen. A hairbrush in Julia Dehning's bathroom takes on as much importance as the Dehning family fortune. The hierarchical order of reality would dictate writing a family history that included only those people and events most central to the family's visible development. But Gertrude Stein was concerned with internal, invisible changes between generations, changes visible solely in terms of what filled the attention field of the character.

One of the most persistent criticisms raised against *The Making of Americans* is its length. It drove Edmund Wilson to write: "I confess that I have not read the book all through and I do not know whether it is possible to do so," and compelled the critic B. L. Reid to proclaim:

> The complete *Making of Americans* is, I am convinced, unreadable for the normal mind. I have read every word of the shorter version (I think I have—it's hard to make sure), but I am not proud of the accomplishment, and I doubt that a score of people could be found to have done even that.[13]

It must be added that Mr. Reid finds most of Miss Stein "unreadable," and the quotation above was taken from his fulllength critical assault on the mass of her creation. Nevertheless Mr. Reid has his point. *The Making of Americans* is not "for the normal mind" if by normalcy we imply conventional. The book assaults our notions of how any book should be organized, let alone stylistically accomplished.

Since there are no hierarchies of reality in Gertrude Stein's universe, not only will all people and objects have the same importance, but all time passages will be of equal significance. Hence absolutely no attempt is made to tell the events of a family history in linear, sequential time (A follow B follows). Time is, rather, seen in terms similar to Henri Bergson's psychological time. When events figure largest in determining character action they seem to exist in mammoth passages of time in spite of the fact that they occur in only a brief passage of ontological time. This tension between actual time and narrative, mental time is illustrated in a memory of Martha Hersland's childhood:

> . . . the one I am now beginning describing is Martha Hersland and this is a little story of the acting in her. . . . this one was a very little one then and she was running and she was in the street

and it was a muddy one and she had an umbrella she was dragging and she was crying. "I will throw the umbrella in the mud," she was saying . . . "I will throw the umbrella in the mud," she was saying, . . . "I will throw the umbrella in the mud," and there was a desperate anger in her; "I have throwed the umbrella in the mud" burst from her, she had thrown the umbrella in the mud and that was the end of it for her.[14]

This marked deceleration in narrative time magnifies a seemingly trivial event several fold. Miss Stein wrote that her favorite novel was Richardson's *Clarissa Harlowe*, and it is perhaps from Richardson that Gertrude Stein learned the technique of occasionally decelerating time to emphasize select action. In any event, the actual act of throwing the umbrella that might have taken Martha five seconds at the most to accomplish is described as if hours or years had passed. The reason for decelerated time is twofold. First, each character reveals himself and his consciousness field by a concrete action that externalizes, brings to the forefront the nature of personal consciousness. This umbrella dumping of Martha is her quintessential response to frustration throughout her entire life. The child is the father of man. When several hundred pages later Martha's marriage to Philip Redfern collapses we can see reverberations from the childhood umbrella incident reverberating in the present. But the link is not a direct association through linear time. The novel is not organized to facilitate such recognizable links through time. In fact the contrary is true. The life events of the characters are so unsequentially arranged that hundreds of pages and thousands of paragraphs might intervene between events in any character's life.

Gertrude Stein maintains this temporal organization because this is her belief in how the human mind remembers and tells family histories. The endless digressions, asides, interminable lists of trivial personalities and banal objects and inconsequential events resemble nothing if not life as we live it daily in America. Daily family living for the middle class in America is Miss Stein's focal interest:

I throw myself open to the public—I take a simple interest in the ordinary kind of families, histories. I believe in simple middle class monotonous tradition.[15]

And if the essence of middle-class living is revealed in monotony and repetition, the essence of American living is disembodiedness, dislocation, temporal discontinuity, unrootedness. The drama between the European quest for roots in the land versus the American attitude is shown in a passage referring to the Hersland grandparents when they were still living in Europe (actually in Germany, a reference omitted from later drafts). Here is the description of the grandparents before they moved across Europe to America:

It was too late now, he had done as his Martha had made him. He would have liked to buy back all that they had been selling. It was very hard to keep him moving. It was hard to start him and it was almost harder to keep him going. How he wanted to settle down again and keep on staying. Perhaps the man who had bought his shop would sell it back to him if they would pay him. "No, David," his wife said to him. "We've got to go now. . . . No, David, don't you see the children are all excited about going. . . ."[16]

Finally all the preparations for leaving the home country are completed. The wife and children climb into the wagon that is filled with their life possessions. But the grandfather walks sullenly beside the wagon. The wagon goes a few miles. The grandfather is nowhere to be found. The wife goes back down the road to find him. She does. They begin their travels again. All these events are told in a highly repetitive, continuous-presence narrative much as Martha's umbrella incident is told. The decelerated time flow stretches the boundaries of the character's quintessential act, and makes it appear more important than it might appear in sequential, ontological time.

A second reason for decelerated time is related to Gertrude Stein's theory of human personality. From our reading of *Three Lives*, we singled out three characteristics of character consciousness that concerned Miss Stein: speed, density, and continuity. When Martha declares. "I will throw my umbrella, etc." she reveals something about the speed of her psychological processes. Not merely that she is slow in some simple-minded way (she is not "slow-minded" in the same way that Doctor Campbell is in *Three Lives*), but that passion is slowly, thoroughly emptied out of her in graduated steps. This gradualness of releasing passion is indicated in her speech patterns: "I will . . . I will . . . I have done."

For Gertrude Stein the "bottom nature" of every character is revealed in the nature of their repetitions. There is a direct correspondence between the rhythm of personality and the sentence rhythm. Every violation of conventional syntax, every word inversion, unqualified dangling clause, every repeated phrase or word is an indicant of consciousness. The changes in the field of consciousness from generation to generation are revealed both linguistically and syntactically. Julia Hersland does not speak like Henry Dehning, who in turn does not sound like his grandfather. It is not that the words they use in their daily discourse are different. The difference is not semantic. In *Three Lives* the two characters argue over the meaning of the words "regular living." The concern in *The Making of Americans* is with the organization of words (which for Miss Stein implies the movement of thought). She declares in her lecture "The Gradual Making of *The Making of Americans*":

I began to get enormously interested in hearing how everybody said the same thing over and over again with infinite variations . . . until finally if you listened with great intensity you could hear it rise and fall and tell all that there was inside them, *not so much by the actual words* they said or the thoughts they had *but the movement* of their thoughts, endlessly the same and endlessly different [my italics].[17]

Consider for a moment how a sentence says what it says. How does the sentence form carry semantic information?

The stock form in Standard American English is subject-verb-object. Our grammar, our conventional organization specifying how words might be related, insists upon the non-reversibility of the subject-object combination in many circumstances. A man climbs a building. A building can't climb a man and so on. Although we rarely consider grammar apart from daily language usage (i.e., a person lacks culture because he uses *ain't*) we might consider grammar as a system that determines how you report a temporal sequence of events.

If we limit our verbal reports of events to the subject-verb-object pattern alone, we find a discrepancy between our perceptual experiences and our verbal reports. To paraphrase William James: while I am typing a fly has flown through my window and my radiator has steamed over. If I am to keep within the limitations imposed by my grammatical model the only way I can convey my perceptual reality is to string together an infinitely long series of subject-verb-object units (this happened, and this, . . . and this). This is exactly what Gertrude Stein does throughout the first half of *The Making of Americans*. Conjunctions abound. But by the David Hersland section conventional syntax is violated entirely. What occurs between the rather conventionally organized (even if intensely overlong) sentences of the opening pages and the asyntactic patterns of the finale is the exhaustion of the conventionally organized sentence in its struggle to recreate consciousness states. Here is Gertrude Stein's own account of this struggle:

> When I was up against the difficulty of putting down the complete conception that I had of an individual, the complete rhythm of a personality that I had gradually acquired by listening seeing feeling and experience, I was faced by the trouble that I had acquired all this knowledge gradually but when I had it I had it completely at one time . . . And a great deal of *The Making of Americans* was a struggle to do this thing, to make a whole present out of something that took a great deal of time to find out. . . .[18]

Another way of stating the problem is this. The perceptual field is always going on. Because we are constantly receiving new knowledge from our senses every second we are always

coming to know what we know. The sentence, the subject-
verb-object matrix, cannot convey the gradualness of coming
into the knowledge of an event. The possibility of revealing psychological process is limited. True, one can link an
indefinite number of sentences together by conjunctions, but
Miss Stein describes well what occurs:

> And my sentences grew longer and longer, my imaginary de-
> pendent clauses were constantly being dropped out, I struggled
> with relations between they them and then, I began with a relation
> between tenses that sometimes almost worked to do it. And I went
> on and on and then one day after I had written a thousand pages
> . . . I just did not go on any more.[19]

A conventionally patterned sentence composed of X number of kernel sentences united by "ands" fails in communi-
cating due to the limited range of human attention spans. By
the fourth page of "and . . . and . . . and . . . " one simply
forgets the initial point of the sentence. No better proof of this
phenomenon can be found than in some of Miss Stein's sentences composed of twenty clauses, at least eighteen dangling.
I would be surprised if she remembered to what even the two
related clauses referred.

The escape from such a dilemma is simply to abandon
conventional sentence patterns. This is exactly what Miss Stein
did by the end of *The Making of Americans*.

Her eccentric punctuation, her play with verb tense, her
clustering of present, active participles are all devices to
achieve the illusion of continual presentness and going-on-ness.
Consciousness is always "going on." Each character has it go
on at a particular speed and density and continuity. But it is
always moving. If writing is to accurately mirror the rhythm
and directions of consciousness how can it do so?

In her lecture "Poetry and Grammar" Gertrude Stein
writes:

> When I first began writing, I felt that writing should go on, I
> still do feel that it should go on but when I first began writing I

was completely possessed by the necessity that writing should go on and if writing should go on what had colons and semi-colons to do with it, what had commas to do with it, what had periods to do with it what had small letters and capitals to do with it to do with writing going on which was at that time the most profound need I had in connection with writing.[20]

So in opposition to the conventionally patterned sentence Gertrude Stein developed her own personal organizations which are more capable of expressing the consciousness as she saw it. The essence of this personal grammar is found in the positional flexibility of various parts of speech. The idea "someone is alive" is converted in the first part of *The Making of Americans* into the phrase "anyone can be a living one." The present participle here indicates the *process* of living. This device is kept throughout the book, but is supplemented by a positional device in the David Hersland section:

> Any one being one being in any family living is being one having been saying something. Any one being one being living is one having been saying something. Any one being in any family living is one having been saying something again.[21]

Try to identify the following parts of speech by their sentence position: "Any"; "one"; and "being."

The paragraph above is nearly void of semantic information. You can paraphrase it by saying: anyone who lives in a family talks. But such a paraphrase misses the point of Gertrude Stein's craft. The final section of *The Making of Americans* describes the youngest member of the Hersland family, David Hersland, Jr. Miss Stein, for reasons known to herself, considers David the "hero" of the novel. At any rate, his consciousness is the most complex, the most intricate, and the most abstract of any character in the novel. Or at least we might surmise these characteristics from the intricacy of the speech patterns used by the narrator to describe David's living. We are told less directly about David than about Martha and Alfred Hersland. We know only that David is "quiet, hard working, understanding that being living is existing" and he "comes to be a dead one" at an early age.

We can only know David Hersland by the movement of words attributed to him by the narrator. We are led to the following situation: what a character says is less significant than *how* he says it. The procress of the mind is reflected in the process of the sentence organizing itself (sentencing itself?). The meaning of individual words matters less than the entire speech flow, for it is the language flow that reflects the passage of consciousness, not any discrete words corresponding to discrete "important" moments in the consciousness flow.

The consequences of a nonhierarchical reality are finally revealed in the book's style as well as in its contents. If all people and objects and events are of equal significance, then all the words used to describe the consciousness of this reality are of equal significance. And if all words are of equal significance then the semantic weight of single words matters less than the plastic arrangement of words in terms of the whole flow. As we will examine in future chapters, this radical reconsideration of the role of words leads to Stein's total abandonment of them as discrete semantic carriers.

Suppose that individual words are no longer used to refer to singular realities but all words are subordinated to the flow in order to expose something about the consciousness flow itself. Once this device is put into practice the possibilities for word organization are nearly endless. The rigidity of word position in the English language is a product of our insistence that language communicate with optimum clarity semantically. We call *celery* a noun, which means that it can be positioned as object in the sentence: Mary eats celery. This positional qualification works quite effectively given the world of our social conventions. Certainly if I parroted Miss Stein and said to a friend: Celery her. Mary her celery. Her Mary celery! my academic career might end in institutional confinement.

But a book such as *The Making of Americans* compels us to question the efficacy of our conventional word organization in describing a non-Aristotelian, psychological, process-centered universe. If you grant Miss Stein's assumptions about personality and consciousness, her stylistic experimentation can be seen as an outgrowth of a writer's attempt to capture life by language, to capture the process of living by recreating English to make it a language more process-oriented.

I think that it is in the paintings of Cézanne that the closest analogy to what Gertrude Stein was attempting in literature can be found. What the French phenomenalist philosopher Merleau-Ponty says about Cézanne applies equally well to Gertrude Stein:

His painting might seem a paradox: a quest for reality without the loss of sensation, without any other guide than nature in its immediacy, without delineating the contours, without framing the color by the drawing, without composing the perspective or the picture itself. This is what Bernard calls Cézanne's suicide: to aim at reality and forbid oneself the means of attaining it.[22]

Substitute the word "consciousness" for "nature," "traditional novel form" for "contours," and "without subordinating consciousness flow to traditional sentence patterning" for "without framing the color by the drawing," and you have a sense of Gertrude Stein's achievement in *The Making of Americans*. I do not share the opinion that Cézanne's technique causes his artistic "suicide" anymore than I share Mr. Reid's opinion that *The Making of Americans* is "unreadable." I think both Cézanne and Stein compel us to drop our conventional assumptions regarding what a painting or novel is. As Cézanne paintings are meta-painting, critiques on painting itself (i.e., what is the purpose of applying color on a white canvas?) so Gertrude Stein's *The Making of Americans* is a meta-novel that makes us question not only the shape of the novel form itself but the nature of the medium, the linguistic "paint" that the writer applies to create a world.

In the works following *The Making of Americans* the experiments into the nature of language become more radical. There are those who consider *Thee Lives* and *The Making of*

Americans Gertrude Stein's last successful artistic ventures. It is because I do not share this belief that I will examine her most radical experiments. Even if Cézanne and Gertrude Stein committed artistic "suicide" we have extensive evidence of their crimes. We may learn from their crimes as well as from their successes.

IV
Tender Buttons:
Beyond Semantics

My aim is to teach you to pass from a piece of disguised nonsense to something that is patent nonsense. . . . He who understands me finally recognizes my propositions as senseless.

—Wittgenstein[1]

Language as a real thing is not imitation either of sounds or colors or emotions it is an intellectual recreation.

—Gertrude Stein[2]

Before we proceed to a consideration of Gertrude Stein's *Tender Buttons* let us consider the literary and historic situation that gave rise to experiments such as Miss Stein's. Since the beginning of the written word writers have delighted in exploring the limits of language. From Shakespeare to Sterne, from Góngora to García Lorca, writers have explored the range of their medium with as much intensity and depth as painters have their palettes. If there is a unique fervor in what we call the modernist age in literature it is the single-mindedness with which our most important authors have tested the limits of their medium. This "medium-consciousness" seemed to occur in several arts simultaneously in the last half of the nineteenth century in Europe. Mallarmé's symbolist poem *"Un Coup de dés . . . ,"* Cézanne's "primitive" landscapes comprised of color patches, and Scriabin's first abstract piano compositions all reflect a new consciousness of one form of art creating another from its own compositional materials. Mallarmé wrote an absolutely meaningless poem as the culmination of his career as a symbolist. It was a fitting act for a poet who maintained a decade earlier that poetry someday would move into pure silence. The symbolist experiment in France represented a foray into the mystic, the ineffable, the inexplicable.

While Mallarmé grew tired of trying to capture the mystery of being in ordinary, shopworn words and syntax, Monet wrote in his diaries: "I grow tired of what appears to be an impossible task. I went down to the lily pond today to capture its transitory beauty. How futile." While Mallarmé struggled with language and Monet with paint, the Russian composer Alexander Scriabin questioned how musical tones could bring about synesthetic, or as we say today, "multi-medianistic experience."

The consequences of such medium experimentation led to the development of art forms that were critiques on art. As we indicated before, a landscape by Cézanne is more than a landscape: it is a penetrating comment on what a painting can or should be. In much the same way Mallarmé's *"Un Coup"* might be read as an essay on perception and corresponding linguistic configurations. One central problem engaged the attention of all the artists mentioned: how can the gulf between what the artist actually perceives and the conventions and tools he uses to record his vision be reconciled. Let us focus upon this problem in the literary realm.

Mallarmé and most of the French symbolists were engaged in describing spiritualistic or neurasthenic states: extreme ecstasy, bliss, terror. They were particularly drawn to descriptions of drowsy, phantasmagorical states of consciousness—Mallarmé had a mystic vision of swans, Rimbaud perceived the hidden beauty of commonplace city trash. Some of the physiological correlations of a drowsy state include a drop in blood pressure, a blurring and graininess of the visual field, and a retardation of neural response. In terms of speech patterns these facts mean slowed, ideationally vague or vapid speech, occasional nonsense or sing-song rhymes. This can be simply tested on yourself. Note how often you awake from a dream with words or phrases that are nonsensical or vague. Although the precise correspondences between this semiconsciousness condition and language usage is not at present fully understood, it is safe to assume that a state of semiconsciousness is reflected in speech in a variety of ways, among them semantic confusion or emptiness, nonsense, singsong, repetition, and verbal playfulness.

Imagine this problem. You are an author writing from the point of view of a character dozing into deep sleep. What techniques can you use to make his drop into sleep convincing? The most commonly used convention has been the use of suspension points to indicate long silences between words ("I think . . . that she . . . will love . . . again," and so on). The suspension points suggest that as sleep approaches the speed of thoughts on the mind is greatly reduced. Thus the

sensation of mental deceleration is crudely represented. But
what of the descent of language into apparent nonsense? What
about the depiction of borderline states between wakefulness
and sleep, where meaningful phrases weave in and out of a
nonsensical speech flow? Considerable skill is required to describe such conditions because to do so the writer must drop
his usual "linguistic set," his usual vocabulary and syntax, and
be willing to use a radically different linguistic "set." For anyone naïve enough to believe that the writing of nonsense is
simple, I suggest they try it themselves. It is painstakingly difficult. The mastery of a Lewis Carroll or an Edward Lear required as much discipline as any other style, possibly more. For
nonsense to capture the adult reader's attention, it must be entertaining and lively. Now what does "liveliness" mean when
we talk about noninformational word groupings?

When I say something to you in the world of everyday
reality, such as "Please pass the butter," neither myself nor the
person passing the butter is particularly concerned with the
aesthetic beauties or psycho-linguistic nuances of the utterances. I want butter, and so I choose and organize my words
in such a manner that I receive the butter in the most expe-
dient, pragmatic way possible. One of the best justifications
for using conventional vocabulary and syntax in everyday life
is that it gets things done. Try to imagine working on a construction crew and giving orders in the jargon of *Finnegans
Wake* or *Tender Buttons*. This linking of conventional language usage and efficacy in dealing with our social reality is
supported by some interesting psychological literature. The
psychotherapist Harry Stack Sullivan discovered in working
with the speech patterns of schizophrenics that the unconventional syntax of psychopaths is traceable to their disillusionment
with the efficacy of conventional language. For most people
language is a tool for the acquisition of desired objects. For
the schizophrenic, personal security, not object satisfaction, is
the goal. Thus the speech of schizophrenics departs from conventional speech, as is illustrated in this example from R. D.
Laing's study of schizophrenia:

JONES: NO, I'm a civilian seaman. Supposed to be high mucka-
        muck society.
SMITH: A singing recording machine, huh? I guess a recording
        machine sings sometimes. If they're adjusted right. Mmhm.
        I thought that was it. My towel, mmhm. We'll be going
        back to sea in about eight-nine months though. Soon as
        we get our—destroyed parts repaired.[3]

Nonsense? Perhaps to an analyst familiar with the case
histories of these two patients the dialogue could be related to
their mental conditions. But let us consider the speech patterns,
both stylistically and aesthetically. Syntax is on the verge of
breaking, conventional words are used in unconventional positions, conventional meaning is minimal.

One of the objections raised to Miss Stein's *Tender Buttons* and later literary efforts is that they mirror the monotony
and meaninglessness of schizophrenic speech. The American
press portrayed Miss Stein as some mad society woman who
simply babbled like a psychopath. I have given this sample of
schizophrenic speech because I wish later to indicate differences between her intentional consciousness fragmentation of
conventional syntax and schizophrenic fragmentation. The
schizophrenic "nonsense" flow contains, however minimal the
number, associational ties between words that presuppose a
consciousness of past life history. Some links between words
are phonemic (seaman/singing); some are intellectual (singing,
recording/singing is a mode of recording); some links are
both phonemic and intellectual (seaman as semen as SEE-
man). All the words might refer to incidents in the patient's
memory. The apparent nonsense of the present speech might
therefore be reducible to semantic comprehensibility by trac-
ing the word referent back into the personal history of the
speaker.

This type of nonsense is certainly in contrast to that of
Lewis Carroll or Edward Lear:

> 'Twas brillig and the slithy toves
> Did gyre and gimble[4] . . .

The issue in the nonsense of Lear or Carroll is not the syntax but, usually, the substitution of conventional meaning with "fanciful" meaning. The syntax is regular. In Gertrude Stein's work or in schizophrenic speech the "non-sense" is created by scrambling elements that are, in themselves, meaningful. One of the remarkable facets of Gertrude Stein's most abstract productions is her insistence upon using a simple and straightforward vocabulary. There are no words in *Tender Buttons* or *Stanzas in Meditation* that could not be understood by an elementary school graduate. But their structurings require the greatest perceptual acumen to unravel.

The question should be raised: why bother to read such nonsense? Why critically examine it? What can be gained by setting it next to schizophrenic speech, automatic writing, or *Alice in Wonderland* except to cast shades upon Miss Stein's sanity or sagacity?

If the thesis of Benjamin Whorf and Edward Sapir is true, if our perceptions of external reality are conditioned by the structure of our linguistic "set," then the exploration of the limits of language, of nonsense, might lead to a novel set of perceptions. A breakthrough in conventional language usage might imply a breakthrough in conventional consciousness.

In psychiatry the work of Sullivan and, most recently, the phenomenological psychology of R. D. Laing suggest that the schizophrenic literally does not perceive the same external reality as does the rest of the population. A chair is not a chair. It is wood, and sticks, and nails, and seat, a place to sit, or perhaps a brother (something sat upon), or a four-legged animal, or a tombstone. Not only may what we call a chair be all these things or have all these qualities, it may be all these things simultaneously! Given the perceptions of a schizophrenic the phrase "please sit in that chair" is void of meaning. Perhaps the phrase "slay their brother leg man" is more accurate.

Research into the perceptual and linguistic development of children also provides valuable material in this regard. The work of Jean Piaget and his colleagues into the language and thought patterns of preschool infants indicates that the child actually perceives a different reality than his parents, and his language uses reflect this difference. Joseph Church, a Piaget follower and theoretician of child psychology, writes in *Language and the Discovery of Reality:*

> Virtually from birth, the child builds up schemata of segments of reality based on his concrete concerns and operations, but it is many years before his bits of knowledge are integrated into any sort of orderly system. Until he comes to inhabit the extended spatial and temporal framework we know as adults, governed by principles and values that transcend particular instances and lend coherence to the conceptual flux in which the young child lives, we cannot expect adult rules of logic to apply. . . . Parents who try to reason with young children often find themselves sinking in a quagmire of rapidly shifting premises, logical inconsistencies, unforeseen implications, word magic, and dissolving obviousness.[5]

This idea of "word magic" is prominent in Bronislav Malinowski's anthropological study of aboriginal savages. Startling as the correspondence might seem initially, Malinowski's aborigines and Church's preschool children both practice a similar variety of word magic.

Church emphasizes the fact that children's word play is a means of testing adult reality. We teach children to speak like ourselves by compelling them to leave their "naïve perceptions." When the child parrots: "May I have some milk, please" and receives it, he comes to link these particular words in this particular order as a formula for success. But even the most obedient of young children love to test language, and will occasionally ask for milk in an inane babble. Such play is often discouraged by parents in this society by: "Stop talking nonsense. Talk like a grown-up and I'll give you your milk." But in spite of parental chagrin, children babble. They invent nonsense games, nonsense dances, play with subvocal sounds, and play with repetition:

> Row, row, row your boat
> gently down the stream
> Merrily, merrily. . . .[6]

They also play with numerical versus ideational sequences:

> One, I love
> Two I love
> Three I love, I say
> Four I love with all my heart
> Five I cast away;

with polymeanings, puns, and entendres:

> a, b, c, d, e, f, g,
> h, i, j, k, l, m, n, o, p,
> q, r, s, t,
> u are out.[7]

with subvocal nonsense:

> Hey nonny, nonny
> hey nonny nonny

and with word scrambles:

> O that I was that I would
> be then I am who was not.

Not only do Malinowski's savage children, as children throughout all world cultures, practice word-game patterns after the above, "pure language constructs for the purpose of entertainment," they also practice operational magic through permutation as do the adult members of their society. Malinowski writes:

> . . . at the very basis of verbal magic there lies what I elsewhere called "the creative metaphor of magic." By this I mean that the repetitive statement of certain words is believed to produce the reality stated. I think if we stripped all magical language to its essentials, we would find simply this fact: a man believed to have mystical power faces a clear blue sky and repeats: "it rains; dark clouds foregather; torrents burst forth and drench the parched

soil" . . . or in illness he repeats, like Monsieur Coué "Every day in every way it is getting better and better." *The essence of verbal magic, then, consists in a statement which is untrue, which stands in direct opposition to the context of reality* [my italics].[8]

I would like to add my own qualifications to the last part of Malinowski's statement. The statements of verbal magic stand in opposition to our socially conventionalized definitions of external reality. The possibility that word magic might actually "work" will be taken up later. The point here is simply that word magic consists of sets of unconventional words and word orders that create in the user or listener the experience of the sought-after object or person. All religions conventionalize their word magics: litanies, chants, hymns, ritual speeches. The aborigine goes one step further. His linguistic development is twofold:

> . . . the individual will find within his culture certain, crystalized, traditional, standardized types of speech with the language of technology and science at one end, and the language of sacrament, prayer, magical formula, advertisement and political oratory on the other.[9]

Certain vocabularies and word organizations are "holy," are powerful enough to induce changes in men and gods. At the very least such numinous word formations are capable of inducing physiological changes in the body of the word magician himself. In *Structural Anthropology*, Claude Lévi-Strauss discussed the primitive religious chant in physiological terms: the chant is so structured as to "drug" the chanter, raise the excitation level of his nervous system, even induce visual hallucination.[10]

If this discussion of word mysticism seems far removed from our everyday lives, I would like for a moment to return to Church's preschool children. I mentioned earlier how the child forms an associational tie between the words "May I have the milk, please," and the receiving of the milk. Freud and his followers discovered that if you deprive a hungry child of milk often enough he will develop hallucinatory methods of deriving satisfaction. Unable to grasp why the repetition of the command: "milk!" fails to bring about the appearance of the desired object, he may break out into babble or tears or sub-vocal play. He may scream the word *milk* for interminable lengths of time, investing the word with gargantuan mystical powers but failing to recognize those factors in reality external to himself that might prevent the milk from being delivered on time. Freud developed a most ingenious and totally un-provable theory for the ontogenesis of the literary artist upon this model: writers suffer various instinctual depivations in their childhoods, and to compensate for their lack of satisfac-tion they play with words and phrases until they can advance to whole stories and literary productions—the roots of which are traceable to the need to create alternative verbal realities in opposition to the socially accepted reality principle.

We have come full circle.

We began our discussion of nonsense with Mallarmé and the symbolists. Some of the most cogent criticisms raised against the symbolists were that they attempted to make a god out of poetry. When Mallarmé talks of a "pure poetry, a po-etry moving toward the voidness of a book of blank pages" (see Chapter VII, Document #12) there is an implicit rejec-tion of conventional reality and a yearning for the beyond. Where the symbolists stopped the surrealists and modernists picked up. Tristan Tzara tells his followers to write poems by clipping words randomly out of a tabloid (See Chapter VII Document #2), mixing them in a paper bag, taking them out while blindfolded, and publishing the result as a poem. André Breton sets down reams of automatic writing without the least intervention of his consciousness. Gertrude Stein insists upon using words as if they never had a history, in combinations never before realized in literature. Suddenly we are faced with a widespread artistic revolution, its implications extending far beyond seminars in modern literature.

The possibility that unconventional language might lead to new areas of consciousness intrigued Gertrude Stein. Unfortunately one is hard put to find the problem explicitly stated in philosophical terminology. Some of her "critical works," particularly *How to Write* and *The Geographical History of America*, discuss the problem, but one must turn to her major literary works for a demonstration of it. I am *not* suggesting that Gertrude Stein was a Wittgenstein and a Whitehead rolled into one. She was simply an American woman in France sensitive to the modernist revolution in the arts, and capable, through intuition and bumbling as well as through intellectual intention, of coming upon certain truths concerning the relations between language and consciousness.

Gertrude Stein lived in a literary period bubbling with linguistic experimentation. Tzara and Hugo Ball's dadaist poems were being published, as were the first dissociated, cubist poetry of that other rich American abroad, Walter Arensberg. Little magazines including *Broom* and *transition* were printing experimental poems by Laura Riding and Mina Loy that, for the *Saturday Post* reader, were as lunatic as those by Gertrude Stein. There was a widespead interest bordering on faddism in mysticism, the East, hypnosis, magic, mythology, Freud, Jung, child perception, drug experimentation. To suppose that Gertrude Stein's work can all be traced back to such intellectual currents is foolish. Allegra Steward, in her ingenuous study *Gertrude Stein and the Present*, attempts just that. She reads *Tender Buttons* as a Jungian mandala embodying various alchemical correspondences. This strikes me as errant nonsense. Testimony from some of those who knew Gertrude Stein best—Carl Van Vechten or Thornton Wilder—support the idea that Gertrude Stein, although a woman intensely aware of the intellectual life about her, was nonetheless her own woman. With a single-mindedness bordering on preposterous megalomania she stubbornly kept writing according to her most singular program.

I have presented the linguistic states of psychopathology, childhood, and primitivism in order to suggest frames of reference through which Gertrude Stein's non-sensical writing can be examined. The criteria of conventional literary criticism cannot function with a book like *Tender Buttons*. I have focused mainly upon psychological and phenomenological issues because I believe Gertrude Stein's later works require and demand this approach. The literature of non-sense can be critically examined and perhaps our appreciation of it can be enhanced by such an examination. But such a critical endeavor must move beyond questions of surface-content analysis.

I would do well to remind the reader that in the dark continent of deepest Stein certain questions are taboo—questions that for years of our literary education we have been taught to treasure: we are geared to think "What does this poem mean?"

And what if it be meaningless?

Would you say, "Don't be ridiculous. Why talk about nonsense?" Consider some "sensical" facts about *Tender Buttons*. It was published in 1914 by the poet Donald Evans in an extremely limited edition. Despite its limited printing the book was Miss Stein's first claim to notoriety. The American press, which had just recovered from its fit of hysterics about the 1911 Armory show, latched onto *Tender Buttons* as being representative of the same spirit as the show. This was "cubistic literature"—for "cubistic" read irrational, untamed, fragmentary, and incomplete. A few astute voices, one of which was that of Sherwood Anderson, recognized *Tender Buttons* as a vital contribution to a new understanding of literary language:

> There is a city of English and American words and it has been a neglected city. Strong broad shouldered words, that should be marching across open fields under the blue sky, are clerking in little dusty dry goods stores, young virgin words are being allowed to consort with whores, learned words have been put in the ditch-digger's trade. . . . For me the work of Gertrude Stein consists in a rebuilding, an entire new recasting of life in the city of words.[11]

What is this slim volume that is responsible, in Anderson's words, for "an entire new recasting of life in the city of words?"

Tender Buttons is a book of definitions divided into three
sections: Objects, Food, and Rooms. Each item to be described
is named in capital letters with the definition listed beneath. In
the Food section, all the items to be described in the section
are listed before individual definitions. It is curious that this
master listing promises descriptions of several items not found
in the text.

But what is most individual and startling about *Tender
Buttons* is that it is a book of object definitions without description. For example, the first object listed appears:

A CARAFE, THAT IS A BLIND GLASS

A kind in glass and a cousin, a spectacle and nothing strange
a single hurt color and an arrangement in a system to pointing. All
this and not ordinary, not unordered in not resembling. The difference is spreading.[12]

It is immediately clear that this is far from a conventional depiction of a carafe. When faced with words and phrases, so
totally removed from conventional usage, one is tempted to
seek out those words that might suggest a carafe. With some
ingenuity such an approach might come up with the following results: a carafe is made of "glass" as are "spectacles." All
glass items have "a single color" (whatever light they happen
to reflect at the moment of observation). What distinguishes
a carafe from other glass objects is its shape: "the difference is
spreading." However ingenious this method of interpreting
Tender Buttons may be, it is an absolutely wrong approach
toward this work. This is one wrong method to handle *Tender
Buttons.*

The second incorrect way of reading the carafe description is to consider it automatic writing. The leading advocate
of this point of view is the behaviorist psychologist B. F.
Skinner:

Miss Stein's description of her experimental results (the automatic writing work at Johns Hopkins) is exactly that of the

average reader confronted with *Tender Buttons* for the first time:
"the stuff is grammatical, and the words and phrases fit together
all right, but there is not much connected thought." In short, the
case is so good, simply on the grounds of style, that we are brought
to the swift conclusion . . . that *Tender Buttons* is written auto-
matically and unconsciously.[13]

There are many refutations of Skinner's thesis. As we will
later show, so-called "automatic writing" as practiced by the
surrealists bears no similarity to the definitions of *Tender Buttons*. But the best refutation of Skinner and the "suggestion"
theories comes from Miss Stein herself in her *American
Lectures:*

I became more and more excited about how words which
were the words that made whatever I looked at look like itself
were not the words that had in them any quality of description.[14]

I want to consider this statement in the light of the whole
body of Gertrude Stein's theory of the artist's mind during
creation. From our discussion of earlier books we discovered
Gertrude Stein's insistence upon the "continuous present," a
presentness of time maintained by a vocabulary and syntax
that is process-oriented. Her approach toward reality emphasized the object "objectifying," or completing itself. Or, in our
own jargon, "you cannot explain a whole thing because if it is
a whole thing it does not need explaining, it merely needs
stating." By the time a writer attempts to describe a waterfall,
a considerable amount of water has fallen over the dam. A
waterfall is a process embodying various qualities (i.e., you
can define a waterfall by the qualities of fall, spray, source
etc.) but what have you said? The discrepancy between what
any particular waterfall is at any one particular moment and
what the dictionary labels a waterfall is immeasurable. Granted,
a lexicographer must give the most broad and economical definition of waterfall, but how can a poet describe one? His description can fit somewhere on a spectrum between literal
description (similar to dictionary definition) and the highly

symbolic or metaphoric. Working within this spectrum of possibilities the vocabulary and syntax will be conventional. Only the farthest reaches of metaphoric expression—a poet likens a waterfall to the pancreas, secretion being the "link"— will entail the use of unconventional descriptive vocabulary.

But the unlikely language of metaphoric expression pre-supposes the recognition of an intellectual key. It implies that the poet's mind at the moment of perceiving the waterfall found an association capable of summing up or clarifying the waterfall experience, of putting it in shorthand.

When Gertrude Stein observes a waterfall or a carafe, returning to our first definition, she is seeking a literal linguistic correspondence to her perception of the object. The key here is time, and it enters into Gertrude Stein's technique in ways alien to conventional descriptive writing. Object: a carafe; say the carafe seen at 4:05 in the afternoon viewed by the authoress in the half-light of her house in Paris is not the same carafe in *Webster's New World Dictionary*. It also differs in kind from every other carafe in literature. It is unmistakably itself. How can this unmistakable carafe be described so as to set it apart from all others. If we resort to conventional definition we must resort to nouns and adjectives: a carafe is an object: a container; a server; a coffee container. The object is: flask-shaped; lightweight; transparent. But what makes Gertrude Stein's 4:05 carafe unique cannot be that which all carafes are. What makes Gertrude Stein's carafe unique is the nature of the carafe as reflected by the describer reflected by the words in the describer's head at the moment of describing the carafe. Michael Hoffman summarizes Miss Stein's concept of the human mind in artistic creation as follows:

The human mind has no emotions, memory, identity or past. It is simply that part of the human consciousness that does nothing but perceive whatever data is immediately available to the senses. The process of writing transfers the knowledge of the human mind to paper as quickly as it is perceived. It has nothing to do with any past knowledge because "the human mind knows what it knows and knowing what it knows it has nothing to do with seeing what it remembers. . . ."[15]

This view of the mind limits its capacity to that of a motion-picture camera. Each second of experience has its corresponding moment in mental time. And in any second of mental time there are words, both in and out of sequence. I would suggest that we call this linguistic cluster in any moment of mental time the "linguistic-moment." For Gertrude Stein, writing represented the conscious, volitional emptying of the words contained in the "linguistic moment." The distinction between Miss Stein's compositions and methods of automatic writing is difficult to establish but valuable to indicate. Automatic writing is the release of the contents of the writer's unconscious mind at the moment of composition without conscious author intervention. As the phrase "automatism" suggests, the conscious attentive stream is frozen, blocked off, so that the locus of attention is directed inward. In Gertrude Stein, the attention, the conscious perceptual apparatus, is heightened in intensity, so much so that synesthesia occurs—she speaks of *Tender Buttons* as the first composition to totally mix sight with hearing with sense. In this moment of heightened perception, words emerge in the mind which are *not* words of conventional semantic correspondence, so that SAUSAGES are:

Sausages in between a glass.
There is read butter. A load of it is managed. Wake a question. Eat an instant, answer.
A reason for bed is this, that a decline, any decline is poison, poison is a toe a toe extractor, this means a solemn change. Hanging.
No evil is wide, any extra in leaf is so strange and singular a red breast.[16]

During the process of heightened perception and word recording only one stylistic imposition or technique is imposed upon the flow. Miss Stein comments in her *Lectures:*

And so in *Tender Buttons* and then on I struggled with the ridding of myself of nouns. I knew that nouns must go in poetry as they had gone in prose *if anything was to go on meaning anything* [my italics].[17]

Because carafes and sausages, cucumbers and rooms, "go on"—move in the writer's consciousness—writing about such objects also must "go on." And if writing is to mirror process-reality, it cannot rely on nouns. Nouns imply objects static in their salient characteristics. This is the point of Miss Stein's difficult essay "Poetry and Grammar." Given her perceptions, given her writer's reality, she insists that writing must "go on," and if it must go on what have nouns to do with it, or adjectives, or commas, or colons, or sentences? The attack upon conventional grammar leads to an attack on conventional typography. *Tender Buttons* continues the premise followed in *The Making of Americans* that the paragraph is the limiting unit. The sentence has lost its function in *Tender Buttons*, so its purpose is no longer informational. The sentence is used as an aesthetic construct rather than as a logical, syntactic necessity. Only the accumulation of such constructs in the paragraph can define the limits of the compositional process.

I was taught in my first "grammar lessons" that one only began a new paragraph when a new "idea" was being presented. In a writing without ideas that utilizes only linguistic "data," the paragraph becomes a purely mechanical method for separating masses of data. For example:

ORANGE

Why is a feel oyster an egg stir. Why is it orange centre.
A show at tick and loosen loosen it so to speak sat.
It was an extra leaker with a sea spoon, it was an extra licker with a see spoon.[18]

The "orange" description above also illustrates a variety of Miss Stein's favorite touches. The nouns used (oyster, orange, centre, leaker) are used in syntactic positions that totally obscure their functions as nouns. This is done with finesse

with the word "orange." In most of the definitions the item
described is not repeated in the lines that follow. When it is,
as in this case, there is an intentional play with nullifying
meaning through syntax. Is an orange centre a reference to a
position of an orange in a still life, or to a centre position colored orange?

This playfulness with concealing semantic correspondences stands at the core of *Tender Buttons*. Even the title reflects this play. Tender buttons? The objects of *Tender Buttons* exist in an obscurity, in a process, in the fantastic, disembodied, unconnected, discontinuous yet concrete world of
everyday reality. Sutherland compares the pieces of *Tender
Buttons* with collages by Gris and the cubists. The analogy is
strong. Nothing belongs together in a Gris collage: its internal
organization is its total lack of cohesiveness, its discontinuity
its only continuity. When we speak of Gris or Gertrude Stein
as being playful, we refer to the movements of the mind
needed to come up with unsuspected juxtapositions of the familiar. Miss Stein makes a great, conscious effort to avoid
familiar word combinations in *Tender Buttons*. Such avoid-
ance of semantic correspondences must imply a conscious
processing of linguistic data. No subject recorded under hypnotic trance, no author of automatic writing, has yet produced
a composition with the particular nuances of *Tender Buttons*.

The author plays with mixing various sense modalities in
her descriptions: veal is described as "very well"—a phrase that
emphasizes the auditory properties of "veal" as a word by slur-
ring the "v" and "w" sounds; "washing"—a phrase that evokes
tactile as well as visionary properties of veal; "cold soup"—
which evokes taste as a property of veal. These peculiar, synesthetic, rhetorical flourishes belong to *Tender Buttons* alone.

For example, there is a prevalent form for object definitions. Under the object name heading an introductory sequence
is given:

VEGETABLE
What is cut. What is cut by it. What is cut by it in.

I was a cress a crescent a cross and an unequal scream, it was upslanting, it was radiant and reasonable with little ins and red.

News. News capable of glees, cut in shoes, belike under plump of wide chalk, all this combing.[19]

The form resembles that of a child's picture book:

PACK HUNTERS

Who is afraid of the big, bad wolf? A moose is. A moose is much bigger than a wolf. He has great horns to help him fight. But he is not safe from the wolf.[20]

This question-and-answer form with rhythms from standard conventional prose is the result of shaping, of much intense listening to the pulse beats of American English. Once the forms and rhythms were mastered by Gertrude Stein, then the syntactic displacements could begin.

One of the side products of such word displacements is the creation of an extraordinary melos, an unheard musical stream of sound. We are unaccustomed to thinking of the music of our speech. But our everyday usages, the manners in which we articulate syllables and words and their proximity to each other in our utterances form a music, a melody. Ezra Pound in *ABC of Reading* defines "Three Powers of Poetry"—the imagistic, the linguistic, and the musical (melopoeia). The melody of our everyday speech is obscured by its semantic carrier. Most of our lives we listen to language for semantic reasons. McLuhan reminds us that we concentrate on one sense to the neglect of the others. Attending to the intellectual weight of words we neglect the phonemic. Words are sounds, and as sounds can be combined to create symphonies; in the same way words can be selected and put next to each other to create sound streams that are symphonies. By removing meaning we attend to sound, and Gertrude Stein is free to create melodies never before possible in English literature because she is liberated from word combinations that most resemble our "everyday musics."

Try reading portions of *Tender Buttons* aloud. Kay Boyle tells of a friend who came close to requiring hospitalization after fits of laughter while reciting *Tender Buttons*. My own experience has been less drastic but nevertheless revealing. The words of *Tender Buttons* have power. They might send a reader into hysteria or set him snoring. But the words removed from their intellectual, semantic straitjackets are as capable of affecting reader emotion as any other words. Perhaps more so. In her *Lectures* Miss Stein writes: ". . . I found I was very much taken with the beauty of the sounds as they came from me as I made them." This discovery of the unexplored sound possibilities and powers of American English resounds through-out the body of her works.

To return to Sherwood Anderson's metaphor the walls of the city of words sounds with a new music. Or, to quote Plato, "when the mode of music changes, the walls of the city shake." William Carlos Williams particularizes Anderson's analogy: Stein has attacked the sacred house of literary language:

Stein has systematically gone smashing every connotation that words have ever had, in order to get them back clean. It can't be helped that it's been forgotten what words are made for. It can't be helped that the whole house has to come down. . . . And it's got to come down because it has to be rebuilt. And it has to be rebuilt by unbound thinking. And unbound thinking has to be done with straight, sharp words. Call them nails to hold together the joints of the new architecture.[21]

We began this chapter with a consideration of nonsense, or nonsemantic communication. The fact that literature that does something other than communicate meaning has power might suggest that there are other qualities besides meaning that draw readers.

A melody of words with the power of Beethoven or Bach to compel men to cry or dance? Just the melody of the words. A nonsensical notion? Look back at the children's word games quoted earlier in this chapter. Some are several centuries old.

What is the basis for their appeal? Or, as William Carlos Williams writes of Gertrude Stein:

It's nonsensical? So are you, only you don't know it. You can't know it without clean words. And you haven't any.[22]

Tender Buttons is a mirror for our nonsense, a dictionary for our daily distraction, a child's first guide to the twentieth century. A symphony for meaning-laden ears. A master score of phenomenology and psychology, naïveté and wisdom, nonsense and sense.

V

Four Saints
in Three Acts:
Play as Landscape

I should like to discourse easily and familiarly on the plot of Stein's piece but must admit that I cannot. The words show evidence of a private playfulness which makes them more difficult to fathom than if they were written under gas.

—Kenneth Burke[1]

Last Act.
Which is a fact.

—Gertrude Stein[2]

When considering *The Making of Americans* we had to reconsider what the novel form implies in terms of the techniques a novelist uses to communicate his message. When examining *Tender Buttons* we had to establish a definition of the elements that comprise descriptive prose.

What is drama for Gertrude Stein, and how does her definition mark a break from the definitions provided by our literary tradition? In her lecture "Plays," Miss Stein traces the roots of her interest in playwriting and supplies us with several highly individual views of the theatrical experience:

> Generally speaking all the early recollections all a child's feeling of the theatre is two things. One which is in a way like a circus that is the general movement and light and air which any theatre has, and a great deal of glitter in the light and a great deal of height in the air, and then there are moments, a very very few moments but still moments. One must be pretty far advanced in adolescence before one can realize a whole play.[3]

Out of all the factors an adult considers when attending a theater the spatial dimensions of the play area are probably the most neglected. After all, why does one attend the theater? For the story of course. And the performance of the actors. And the insights into the human condition. And to laugh or cry or to "forget ourselves." But we are drawn into William James's perception theory again: what do we attend to most intensely in our perceptual field? Consciousness is always necessarily consciousness of something to the neglect of something else in the field. I believe that most of us attend plays with the plot primarily in mind. What we chiefly attend to is the direction of the plot, which, throughout our literary tradition, implies a dramatic movement toward resolution of action, catharsis, climax. Needless to say, there are thousands of variations on this pattern of dramatic action. A dramatic climax for Aristotle is not the same for Racine or Shakespeare or Shaw. I am insisting only on the central reality of plays in our tradition as movement of character action. In the most elemental terms: things happen on stage in a progression toward greater disclosure of information. Eventually, sometime during the play's course of events, information is given that allows the audience to synthesize earlier disparate bits of data. A key is given to the movement of the characters. A plot is discovered. The dramatic action is resolved. In this most simplified and skeletal view of theater we can consider most dramatic productions prior to the twentieth century.

In the twentieth century this elemental model breaks down. One of the primary model breakers was Gertrude Stein. Her attack upon this conventional notion of drama begins with her recollection of trips to the playhouse, quoted earlier.

She reminds us that all plays take place in a highly particularized space. A play is, first of all, that which takes place behind a curtain, on a stage frontally located apart from the audience. The play is something presented for the consideration of an audience. But considerably more may be presented for an audience's consideration than dialogue. Take for example the fact of the actors' presence, the setting, the lighting, the curtain. These elements are usually considered secondary and subordinate to the message. But must they be?

For Gertrude Stein the stage area is analogous to a circus ring. Things happen at a circus: clowns go through their paces, horses and bears prance, the ringmaster shouts. And yet ask a child who has attended a circus for the first time in his life what happened, what was it like? and his answer will probably follow Miss Stein's. We remember the atmosphere of the tent. We remember clowns and buffoons not merely for their slapstick but for their costumes, makeup, and postures. The circus is an area of magical possibilities sealed off from objective reality. It is a particularized area with "a great deal of glitter in the light and a great deal of height in the air."

"And then there are moments," Miss Stein reminds us.

These moments at the circus are when a fusion of atmosphere and action occurs, when the magic of the arena becomes actualized, when the clowns in costume enter the imaginations of the audience in suits.

I risk repeating the obvious to emphasize Gertrude Stein's concept of theater. Her theater turns away from naturalism to enter a realm of high fantasy or romance. Rather than attempting to simulate social reality on stage, she uses her talents to create an alternative, imaginative reality. This alternative reality is created entirely through verbal magic and setting.

Keeping this frame of reference let us consider *Four Saints in Three Acts*. Whatever else the play is it is a landscape—which implies the following: the area on stage is "Spain" (though certainly not in a naturalistic Spain grounded in history). There are the following objects in "Spain": saints —forty at my last count, in spite of the title—pigeons, magpies, fish. The title, the play notwithstanding, occurs in dozens of acts. In fact the conventional categories of acts and scenes serve as a parodying device much as the chapter divisions of Sterne's *Tristram Shandy* do. Not only is the play a conscious effort to seriously redefine drama but it is also a humorous thrust at the oldtime "well-made play."

The play became the text for an opera with music composed by Virgil Thomson.[4] Although my remarks about *Four Saints* consider it primarily as a play, it is worth keeping in mind that this was a play sung by characters. That the entire cast of the opera was Negro was a most unusual facet to a play with absolutely no connections with Negro life. Virgil Thomson writes that an all-Negro cast was chosen "purely for beauty of voice, clarity of enunciation, and fine carriage." With due respect for Mr. Thomson's honesty another reason for an all-Negro cast might have been the spectacle created by their presence. There is something of a Barnum & Bailey flavor to a play about Spanish saints taking place on a stage with scenery composed entirely of cellophane, performed by an all Negro-cast choreographed to move like Balinese dancers.

Add to this spectacle Miss Stein's text:

>To know to know to love her so.
>Four saints prepare for saints.
>It makes it well fish,
>Four saints it makes it well fish.[5]

The language of the play is a composite of Gertrude Stein's styles of the past three decades. Relatively straight-forward lines are combined with hermetic ones. For example:

>Four saints were not born at one time although they knew each other. One of them had a birthday before the mother of the other one the father. Four saints later to be if to be if to be if to be if to be one to be. Might tingle.[6]

One of the styles used widely throughout *Four Saints* is the "cut-up" method, which has not been previously discussed in this book. In Miss Stein's movement from an idiosyncratic but nevertheless naturalistic style to the cubistic lines of *Tender Buttons* an intermediary style arose. Snips, or cutcups from everyday conversation were removed from their total speech flow and arranged architectonically. For instance, this brief section from a short prose composition of the 1920s:

PAGE II

>What did you say about women.
>Were you angry.
>Do you mind.
>Can you feel a discrimination.
>Can you be harsh.[7]

Here each phrase makes perfect sense within itself but the accumulation of such phrases, often trivial in meaning, tends to render the cluster meaningless. Many of the cut-outs consist of selections from high society or ladies' tea parties, and are fascinating as exhibitions of the vapidity and mental sloth of such circles:

>Can a Jew be wild
>. . . . . . .
>Can you speak.

The dog.
Can you bear to tear the skirt.

. . . .

I cannot find a real dressmaker.
Neither can I.[8]

Entire scenes of *Four Saints* consist of these cut-outs reproduced verbatim with an occasional reference to Spain or
saints to keep some local color in the play:

SCENE II

It is very easy to love alone. Too much too much. There are
very sweetly very sweetly Henry very sweetly Rene very sweetly
many very sweetly. They are very sweetly many very sweetly
Rene very sweetly there are many very sweetly.

There is a difference between Barcelona and Avila. What
difference.[9]

The play does focus its attention between Barcelona and
Avila in a spiritual sense: the two chief characters in the play
are Gertrude Stein's favorite saints: Saint Therese of Avila and
Saint Ignatius Loyola. The two saints have much in contrast
with each other: male, female; passive suffering, active suffering; humility and grandeur. But within the play we are not
dealing with the historical saints of the Church tradition. We
are faced with saints that are Miss Stein's personal creations:

In Four Saints I made the Saints the landscape. All the saints
that I made and I made a number of them because after all there
are a number of things in a landscape all these saints together made
a landscape . . . A landscape does not move nothing really moves
in a landscape but things are there. . . .[10]

Saint Therese and Saint Ignatius are stage props: talking
stage props. Their importance to the play is simply that they
do most of the talking. There are dozens of saints that are silent
for the duration of the play. Their appearance is justified by
what they contribute to the set, the landscape. Here we see a
possible reason for Miss Stein's choice of saints as a play sub-

ject. Donald Sutherland writes: "A saint, whether he does anything or not, exists in and with the universe and shares its life,
sustained in existence by the general miracle of the present
world."[11] I find Sutherland's remark directly to the point. A
saint need not do anything but exist in order to create an aura,
an atmosphere about himself. A saint is defined by the quality
of his presence, his ability to be within the world and at the
same moment transcend it:

> If it were possible to kill five thousand chinamen by pressing
> a button would it be done.
> Saint Therese not interested.[12]

This saintly mixture of worldknowingness and other-
worldliness can be found plentifully in Gertrude Stein. Having
lived through two world wars she writes about war with the
same naïveté and lightness as she does about an Alice B. Toklas
dinner. This quality of absolute indifference toward the world
of political and social responsibilities infuriated many of her
fellow writers. But perhaps they failed to realize how closely
Miss Stein kept the saint figure as an ideal.

A saint is a traveler between two worlds: earth and
heaven. One result of traveling both kingdoms is that a saint
learns to speak both with the languages of men and angels:

> Tangle wood tanglewood.
> Four saints born in separate places.
> Saint saint saint saint.
> Four saints an opera in three acts.
> My country 'tis of thee sweet land of liberty
>   of thee I sing.[13]

From this most American-jargonized saint talk we move
to the grand, mysterious sounding litanies of:

> All Saints. Any and all Saints. All Saints. All and all Saints.
> All Saints. All in all Saints. All Saints. All Saints. All Saints. Saints
> all in all Saints. All Saints. Settled in all Saints. All Saints.[14]

What does all this mean? What distinguishes the word clusters of *Four Saints* from all the earlier experiments we have examined? I believe that *Four Saints* can be set apart from Miss Stein's other creations in the following manner. *Four Saints* is a circus. We are confronted not by performing clowns but by talking saints. As clowns are run through their paces so these saints unleash their bag of verbal games and plays. What is presented to the play's audience is a set of verbal games and musical statements that the spectator might enter into and play for himself. Valéry's remark that someday literature will exist only as entertaining games comes to mind. The audience is presented with a landscape to gaze upon ("the glitter in the air") and words to dazzle, to confuse, to delight. Among the games presented are:

ILLOGICAL REPETITIONS:

Four saints are never three.
Three saints are never four.
Four saints are never left altogether.
Three saints are never left idle.[15]

COUNTING GAMES:

One two three four five six seven all good children go to heaven some are good and some are bad one two three four five six seven.[16]

GRADUATED SYNTACTIC DISPLACEMENT:

To be interested in Saint Therese fortunately.
To be interested in Saint Therese fortunately.
Saint Ignatius to be interested fortunately.
Fortunately to be interested in Saint Therese.[17]

PHONEMIC PLAY:

Saint Therese.	When.
Saint Settlement.	Then.
Saint Genevieve.	When.
Saint Cecile.	Then.
Saint Ignatius.	Men.[18]

> Pigeons on the grass alas.
> Pigeons on the grass alas.[19]

All of these verbal structures are woven into a larger fabric for a most surprising reason. Miss Stein distinguishes this play from the conventional, naturalistic drama in this manner:

> Your sensation as one in the audience in relation to the play played before you your sensation I say your emotion concerning the play is always either behind or ahead of the play at which you are looking and to which you are listening. So your emotion as a member of the audience is never going on at the same time as the action of the play.[20]

The issue of dramatic presentation for Miss Stein involves the synchronization of dramatic movement with audience passional response. This issue of synchronizing actor action with audience response is not considered by most playwriters as a problem. Indeed, what is usually called "dramatic tension" in a play by Shakespeare or Shaw is the very want of synchronized action Gertrude Stein complains about! The actors in such plays are always one step ahead of the audience, which implies the possibilities of surprising the anticipations of the audience. But such a lack of synchronized action and audience response also gives the conventional drama an aura of the past. The play is reenacted, implying that the actions of the play actually occurred in one stretch of past time and they are being acted *again* in present stage time.

Gertrude Stein sought to infuse her plays with the same state of presentness and immediacy that informed all her other compositions. How could a play exist totally in the present consciousness of the audience? The first step would entail the elimination of plot. If nothing happens but talking there is no worry about distinguishing past from present. If the play is nothing more than landscape, landscapes change little over long stretches of time, particularly if they are landscapes grounded in the Spanish countryside. In a setting with minimal change and movement there is an atmosphere of timelessness.

Into this timeless arena saints speak. What the saints say is also timeless. Games and riddles, verbal melodies and textures, need no precise temporal or spatial context in which to exist. It is when words are considered primarily for their semantic carrier that they seem dated. The words "one two three four five six seven" formed a melody for Shakespeare as well as for Gertrude Stein. Although the period from Shakespeare to Miss Stein has witnessed the variation or loss of the original meaning of thousands of words, the ability of the words to be sounded as musical tones has remained constant. There is nothing iconoclastic in Miss Stein's use of verbal games and music in drama. How different is Shakespeare's "Hey nonny, nonny, no" nonsense refrain from Gertrude Stein's "pigeons on the grass alas"? The issue is one of emphasis. Gertrude Stein chooses to create entire plays composed solely of these constructs.

So the effort to involve the audience in *Four Saints* focuses upon the audience's willingness to enter the author's consciousness through her verbal games: a three-ring circus of saints' singing games. Yet, while listening to the recording of the opera, I discovered that parts of the play seem to "move" faster than others. How is this possible in an actionless play? An answer might be that some verbal games are denser, more for the audience to ponder than others. Anyone can follow the counting games. But the plays with word positioning through long sequences are slower to adjust to. So the conventional categories of accelerated or decelerated dramatic action are replaced by games of lesser and greater verbal density. Dramatic tension is created by the contrasts between different verbal masses. Some scenes consist of only one word repeated three times. Others comprise scores of lines filled with the most intricate varieties of verbal embroidery. Set in contrast with each other they create tensions analogous to the color of painted masses in Kandinsky or Pollock.

One final comment is in order concerning *Four Saints*. Like any circus it is great fun. The whimsy and nonsense of much of the play is handsomely complimented by Virgil Thomson's simple and popular-sounding score. There is something basically absurd about the play, absurd in terms that are congenial to such contemporary absurdist playwrights as Samuel Beckett and Eugene Ionesco. The lack of character movement, the play as static landscape, the nonsensical talk, and the verbal, gamelike qualities with which Gertrude Stein shocked 1934 audiences have become commonplaces to 1970 audiences accustomed to *Waiting for Godot* and *The Bald Soprano*. But Miss Stein prophesied this direction for the theater,[21] and prophesied her own role as an artist bringing about this revolution:

That is the reason why the creator of the new composition in the arts is an outlaw until he is a classic. . . .

For a very long time everybody refuses and then without a pause everybody accepts.[22]

VI
Stanzas
in Meditation:
A Phenomenology
of Mind

I have begun to think everything.

—Gertrude Stein

Take any concrete finite thing and try to hold it fast. You cannot, for so held, it proves not to be concrete at all, but an arbitrary extract or abstract which you have made from the remainder of empirical reality. The rest of things invades and overflows both it and you together, and defeats your rash attempt. . . . In the end nothing less than the whole of everything can be the truth of anything at all.

—William James[1]

In the early 1930s Gertrude Stein began work on a long philosophical poem that was to mark the pinnacle of her experiments with the language/consciousness problem. It was completed in 1933, but was never published in the author's lifetime. Yale University released it in its collection of Miss Stein's posthumous, unpublished writings twenty-five years after its completion. This poem, *Stanzas in Meditation*, is at the present time the most neglected of Gertrude Stein's major compositions. With the exception of Donald Sutherland's introduction to the Yale edition—and even the most perceptive Mr. Sutherland appears stymied by it—there is no criticism concerning it. Upon initial readings it appears as the most obscure production of the modernist movement. While *Tender Buttons* gave clues as to possible readings (subject titles before defining paragraphs) *Stanzas* supplies the intrepid reader with an absolute minimum of clues.

The poem is divided into arbitrary "parts" and stanzas. There are no thematic links between stanzas or between lines within a stanza. There is no coherent, thematic development in any collection of stanzas that comprise a "part." It is, in fact, extremely difficult to detect even the grammatical subject of dozens of stanzas. Only one specific subject is mentioned in the work and that not until the final section. The most common subjects are nebulous: "He"; "She"; "They." There appears to be no justification for calling the poem philosophical, for there are no occurrences of ideas, and no philosophical terminology or structural formation contributing to the presentation of philosophical thought. The task of explication appears hopeless unless we look beyond the text itself and examine the underlying patterns of the author's more accessible work.

The most specific aid we can bring to an examination of *Stanzas* is the corpus of Gertrude Stein's philosophical assumptions that rest behind her compositional methods. It has been my contention throughout this book that Gertrude Stein's literary work represents an attempt to capture James's pluralistic universe through the development of an experimental syntax. Conventional English syntax compels its user to accept the model of a sequential, linear time/space realm that is not true to the modern, post-Heisenburgian world view. One of the most curious of psychological phenomena that conventional syntax tends to screen out from everyday, individual consciousness is the phenomenon of *simultaneity*.

As we discussed earlier in our definition of consciousness density, simultaneity is the experience of sensing two or more mental phenomena simultaneously in any one given moment of consciousness. As Marshall McLuhan notes in *The Gutenburg Galaxy* it is precisely this experience of simultaneity that literature on the printed page threatens. The meaning of any group of words that comprise a sentence on a printed page is limited to the meaning the typography imposes upon the words. In other words, the meaning of any sentence is the meaning as derived from the sequential, left-to-right collection of discrete units of information. The acceptance of a sequential, unit by unit, semantic synthesis of the discrete units is implicit in the act of comprehending the printed sentence.

Imagine for the moment that a magnetic force field, either positive or negative, attractive or repulsive, surrounded each word in the language. In conventional speech the power and sign ($\pm$) of the field is dependent on the variety of intelligible semantic combinations. An intelligible communication—say, "John left early for work"—functions to communicate one thought by matching words of complementary field forces and strengths. The first word of the utterance is the subject, the initiator of the action. The second word supplies the type of action. And so on, left to right, the words are so arranged that the sequential collection of them supplies a precise message.

I would like to consider what happens to sentence formation when the force fields are uncomplementary and unsequential. Given this five-word combination—"John left early for work"—and all the possibilities of scrambling offered by it, we probably could not eliminate some hint of the semantic carrier. The most unintelligible combination would probably be: "left work early John for." Semantic intelligibility has not been lost because there are still a few words that maintain, even in disjuncture, the "glow" of the original field relation. But what is introduced in the new combination is a maximum of semantic *ambiguity*. The words could be unscrambled to create an entirely new utterance: "John left for early work."

In Miss Stein's earlier compositions, such as *Tender Buttons,* the positional scrambling was so arranged that all possibility of semantic clarity, of setting the sentence "right" again, was reduced. For example:

MILK

Climb up in sight climb in the whole utter needles and a guess a whole guess is hanging. Hanging hanging.[2]

This reduction of meaning to the point at which all possibility of setting the sentence right is reduced to nil is in keeping with the compositional and philosophical aim of *Tender Buttons*. The description consists of a moment in the subjective continuum of the writer that corresponds to the moment of the visual perception of the object. In that moment, the words that came to Miss Stein's mind were disjointed, disembodied, unassociated, not the conventional descriptive words associated with the object in everyday discourse. In *Tender Buttons* the Jamesian universe of flux and process is dramatized by the processual syntax; the description, the verbal embodiment of the object, is as plastic, as multidimensional and as protological as objective reality itself.

In *Stanzas* a different approach prevails, both toward objective reality and the linguistic embodiment of it. Instead of scrambling sentence elements to eliminate the possibility of intelligible recombination the very opposite technique is employed: the central device of the poem is the conscious maximizing of semantic possibility. Each line of each stanza contains multiple options of readings. Each stanza, therefore, also contains multiple readings and so on through each part.

But unlike Joyce's *Finnegans Wake,* all of these multiple readings contain an extremely low-grade semantic carrier. For example, consider Stanza III in Part I:

It is not now that they could answer
Yes and come how often
As often as it is the custom
To which they are accustom
Or whether accustomed like it
In their bought just as they all
Please then.[3]

The first line can be stated: "It is not now that they could answer" or "It is not now that they could answer/Yes" or "It is not now. That they could answer/Yes and come." . . . We spoke earlier of the graduated displacement of conventional syntax. In Miss Stein's earlier poetry this displacement occurred over a span of lines. What has occurred in *Stanzas* is the same method extremely concentrated. Each line contains all the syntactic variants previously contained in separate poetic lines. The reader of the lines creates, or, rather, reenacts the poem by focusing his attention on the multiplicity of word connections both within and beyond the individual line.

A key to the discovery of this method is given by Gertrude Stein in her *Geographical History of America:*

I found that any kind of a book if you read with glasses and somebody is cutting your hair and so you cannot keep your glasses on and you use your glasses as a magnifying glass and so read word by word makes the writing that is anything something[.][4]

By placing an equal perceptual stress on the perception of each word the conventional ideational hierarchy behind conventional syntax is rejected. When each word of an utterance is subjected to its own, individual moment of magnification no noun conventionally labeled as sentence subject is any more important than any article or conjunction. Each word in an utterance emits a glow, a force field equal to that of any other word. So the possibilities of multiple linkages between words is intensified. Such words in a poetic line establish "territories" or "zones" of semantic intelligibility. But since the words chosen to fit into the lines of *Stanzas* are the simplest of pronouns, articles, and conjunctions—words intentionally chosen for their limited field of semantic reference—the multiple readings generate a multiplicity of apparently trivial and commonplace utterances, often to the determined reader's chagrin.

To demonstrate the dynamics of this technique consider the first dozen lines of Stanza XV in Part I:

> Should they can be they might if they delight
> In why they must see it be there not only necessarily
> But which they might in which they might
> For which they might delight if they look there
> And they see there that they look there
> To see it be there that they look there
> Which may be where where it is
> If they do not occasion it to be different
> From what it is.
> In one direction there is the sun and moon
> In the other direction there are cumulous clouds and sky
> In the other direction there is why
> They look at what they see[.][5]

A quick gloss might give the following reading: they might find delight if they choose to observe the landscape. One might call this the "theme" statement. Contrapuntal variations on the theme are given by the minute variations discovered in reading all the possibilities of each line. For example, the first two lines can be read with at least six different stressed word patterns (read the lines emphasizing "should," "they," "can," "delight," each individually).

The effect is like that of a three-dimensional image: objects stand in relief off the surface of a flat plane. Or one is reminded of the multifaceted structures of Gestalt psychology: the cube that changes faces at an eye's blink. The poem's multidimensionality catches the reader with surprise for much the same reason as does the Gestalt cube: a seemingly conventional blatant form, when subjected to depth perception, reveals itself not to be conventional and straightforward at all. The poem's metric (which Donald Sutherland aptly names "a very plain iambic affair") is hardly distinguishable from that of a dozen other long English poems. On the page the poem looks like a reverie by Wordsworth or Robert Bridges. All the classical rhetorical devices of the English long poem—symmetry both within and without the line, antithesis—are used but subverted by Miss Stein, who turns them inside out to suit her own purposes. Despite its surface appearance the poem's preoccupation with revealing its multidimensionality marks it as a most singular experiment in the long poem tradition.

Moving from the cube of Gestalt psychology to the cube of cubism, we find that the strongest analogy to the poetic line with multiple reading inherent in its structure lies in modern art. It is not coincidental that the only precise subject reference of the entire poem is to the surrealist artist Francis Picabia. Gertrude Stein writes of him in *The Autobiography of Alice B. Toklas:*

. . . Picabia had conceived and is struggling with the problem that a line should have the vibration of a musical sound and that this vibration should be the result of conceiving the human form and the human face in so tenuous a fashion that it would induce such vibration in the line forming it. It is his way of achieving the disembodied. It was this idea that conceived mathematically influenced Marcel Duchamp and produced his The Nude Descending the Staircase.[6]

Allegra Steward's study of Miss Stein perceptively picks up this notion of vibration and uses the term in reference to Miss Stein's syntax:

If we study her work carefully we can see that from 1910 on, at least, it was her purpose to exhibit words afresh; to dissociate them from conventional context and stale association, and thus to display them with more of their power and capacity for vibration

—more, in short, of their *being*. Now vibration occurs when a word conveys simultaneously two or more of its meanings each of which is relevant to the context. . . .[7]

This "vibratory syntax" occurs elsewhere in the Gertrude Stein corpus (we noted an example in the David Hersland section of *The Making of Americans*) but in *Stanzas* it functions almost solely as a unifying technique.

What does all this insight into the poem's structure mean? One of the enormous paradoxes evident in the reading of *Stanzas* is that the discovery of technique does little to open the poem to exposition. Once the key to this possible reading is explored the reader is left with several most central questions: what is this poem about and what justification does it have for its existence other than as a magnificent tour de force of ornate syntax? As a philosophical poem what does it reveal of Gertrude Stein's philosophy and its relation to that of James, Whitehead, and Santayana?

I began this analysis of *Stanzas* by emphasizing the poem's syntactic structure because it is through this structure that the philosophy of the poem is enacted. It is my contention that the poem is not *about* philosophy, but *is* philosophy set into motion by verbal action. The philosophy of the poem occurs in the act of reading the text.

Consider the actual information related through the body of the poem itself. The one recognizable voice of the text is that of Miss Stein herself. Stylistically this is evident through the vibratory syntax, the phonemic play, and phonemic repetition. In terms of content she reveals her identity through phrases such as: "I have my wellwishers thank you" and "In each generation there are so few geniuses/Why should I be one." She comments throughout on the difficulty of composition (reminiscent of her intervention in the narrative of *The Making of Americans*) with phrases like "I wish to remain to remember that stanzas go on" and "Thank you for hurrying through." So we might assume the "I" of the poem refers to Gertrude Stein. As for the endless "hes" "shes" and "theys" we might consider them acquaintances and fellow artists of her Paris circle during the first two decades of this century. Such speculation might be supported by the activities of these nameless pronouns. They seem to enjoy traveling, gazing at landscapes, going to parties. In fact, the endless choruses of referential-less pronouns almost seems a mockery of cocktail-party chatter or gossip heard in the dusty back room of Shakespeare & Co. An additional support for the belief that the pronouns represent her fellow artists is that the only specific reference in the poem is to Picabia who, along with Francis Rose and Pavel Tchelitchew, engaged Gertrude Stein's artistic interest at the time this poem was written.

Granting the likelihood that these persons appear in *Stanzas*, we are still left with the question of what happens in the poem, where does it occur, and how. As to what happens— nearly nothing. Characters talk and utter commonplaces, go here and there, and disappear in and out of the narrative. One can speculate with some certainty as to where the action occurs. At the time of writing Gertrude Stein was living in Bilignin, in Southern France, and these otherwise sparse, intellectual, imageless verses are occasionally charged with the imagery of this romantic landscape; imagery that will later become the backdrop for *Lucy Church Amiably* and *Mrs. Reynolds:*

> Here I only know that pumpkins and peas do not grow
> Well in wet weather
> And they think kindly of places as well as people[.][8]

Stanzas are filled with hay, straw, barnyard life of every kind, as well as particularly precise descriptions of sky and sun. These images stand out in bold relief in a poem so lacking a conventional frame of reference.

So we have placed our subjects and their actions in a context. I can imagine the complaints of the reader who has persevered thus far: "You mean to imply that this overelaborated, hypersyntaxed, attenuated description of Gertrude Stein and

her coterie basking in Bilignin warrants this prolix an exposition and is a 'major work' of her career?"

As we have noted in her other works, *Stanzas* is less important for its actual content than for its craft and for what
that craft reveals about the language/consciousness question.
Apples were painted centuries before Cézanne. We pay Cézanne homage for the peculiarity of his vision of apples as
transfixed in paint. And so with Gris's guitars, Duchamp's
nudes, Picasso's clowns. It is the peculiar revelation of multidimensionality in an object previously seen in a conventional
manner that these artists deliver. We return constantly to the
importance of vision to the twentieth-century artist: the disembodied, fragmentary, discontinuous vision of the cubists
united with the organic, processual vitalism of James and
Whitehead. These currents combine in the figure of Gertrude
Stein, and *Stanzas* reveals the results of such fusion.

Stanzas in Meditation: just what comprises the meditative
strain in Gertrude Stein and what relevance does it hold in
terms of the poem's philosophical import? Consider the dilemma
of the creative artist in the following terms: the writer can
choose allegiance to one of two worlds—he can either take the
socially accepted objective reality and use it as the "stuff" of
his writing, or he can attempt to create an alternative, aesthetic
reality. We considered this issue in our discussion of the symbolists. Mallarmé attempted to create a poetry which stood as
an alternative reality, a self-sufficient realm of aesthetic value
in opposition to the accepted social reality. Clearly this is a
simplification of a vast problem. Zola and Céline are both
called "realists." Yet it is arguable whether or not they both
inject substantial doses of fantasy into their narratives under
the guise of sounding "realistic." Nevertheless there is an entire spectrum of difference between the Mallarmés on the one
hand and the Zolas and Célines on the other.

One of the problems of holding to Mallarmé's position is
the difficulty, perhaps the impossibility, of shutting oneself off
from the world, of anathematizing one's responses to the given,
objective reality. But it is my belief that this is precisely the

thrust of Gertrude Stein's activity. Consider these two statements, the first by Allegra Steward, the second by Thornton Wilder:

> There is testimony to the fact that she practiced meditation. Thornton Wilder . . . tells us in his introduction to *Four in America* that Gertrude Stein had an impressive habit of meditating every day. He makes it clear, however, that he speaks of meditating in the sense of vigorously pursuing a certain train of thought for an hour or two at a time; and he does not tell us whether her meditations carried her over the psychic border.[9]

Wilder writes:

> It has often seemed to me that Miss Stein was engaged in a series of spiritual exercises whose aim was to eliminate during the hours of writing all those whispers into the ear from the outside and inside world where the audience dwells.[10]

If we replace the term "spiritual exercises" with "psychological and aesthetic exercises" we will capture the root of Gertrude Stein's concern in *Stanzas*. Much as spiritual exercises are trials for the purpose of preparing the initiate for turning away from a lower plane of reality in order to seek the highest plane, so these poems are psychological exercises that compel the reader to drop his objective-worldliness and enable him to enter the aesthetic and psychological universe of the poem. Meditation for Gertrude Stein represented a method of shutting out external reality.

Wilder's explanation of what meditation meant to Gertrude Stein can be well supported by summarizing her pre-literary as well as her literary career. As a psychology student she was concened with automatism (the total shutting out of the perception of external reality so that the internal constituents of consciousness might be examined). From Melanctha of *Three Lives* to the still lifes of *Tender Buttons*, her literary career centered upon the effort to utilize a syntax most evoca-

tive of the true nature of things as she endlessly pondered them
in her isolated consciousness.

The key question, repeated endlessly throughout her *Lectures in America*, *How to Write*, and *Geographical History* is:
How do I, as a writer, come to know of the world what I
know? It is helpful to read these expository, critical works less
as literary criticism than as personal tracts on epistemology
and the phenomenology of the mind. She is fascinated by the
nature of knowing a person or object through all its permutations in time, and developing a literary technique that transfers
this gradualness of knowing back to the reader:

> I began writing the portraits of any one by saying what I
> knew of that one as I talked and listened that one, and each time
> I talked and listened that one I said what I knew they were then.
> . . . Every time I said what they were I said it so that they were
> this thing, and each time I said what they were as they were, as I
> was, naturally more or less but never the same thing each time that
> I said what they were I said what they were I said what they were
> I said what they were, not that they were different nor I was different but as it was not the same moment which I said I said it
> with a difference.[11]

This extreme sensitivity to the most minute changes of
reality in process could only come about, paradoxically
enough, through a determined isolation from direct perceptual
activity. In everyday conversation we are simply too caught
up in the exigencies of the content itself to notice the peculiar
permutations of our speech patterns. Too many externals are
pressing upon the situation, preventing us from focusing exclusively upon personality change as revealed through speech-
pattern change through time. But if I enter an isolation chamber where only my own voice can be reproduced I might be
compelled to notice speech characteristics this minute. Subjects under hypnosis or in a drug-induced coma whose perception of present external reality is reduced report an intensified awareness of speech patternings. It is only when speech
can be focused upon as an isolated object for introspection

that one's awareness of the gradualness of syntactic change can be intensified dramatically.

I am suggesting that this is exactly what Gertrude Stein accomplished in *Stanzas*. She forced herself to focus upon bits of commonplace conversation and put them through all their conceivable syntactic combinations until they emitted a glow and, like the still lifes of *Tender Buttons*, became transformed from dully perceived commonplace to objects for aesthetic contemplation. The vibratory syntax in *Stanzas* represents nothing more than a revelation into how the human mind meditates upon reality—through the endless coming to terms with its changes. Consider this idea in the light of Stanza Thirteen in Part V:

> There can be pink with white or white with rose
> Or there can be white with rose and pink with mauve
> Or even there can be white with yellow and yellow with blue
> Or even if even it is rose with white and blue
> And so there is no yellow there but by accident.[12]

Part of any object to be contemplated remains itself through time while other elements vary. The rose as flower is, at the same moment of perception, the color rose, and contemplation of the rose leads to contemplation of all the spectrum colors that can combine to produce the shade of rose. The stanza above describes the flower subjected to depth perception: the rose meditated upon until its constituent elements vibrate and glow. The effect is not unlike Wallace Stevens's description of a nightgown's color variations in *Disillusionment at Ten O'Clock:* the object's color appears disembodied from the object's structure, seems to hover about the object like a halo or haze. The halo represents a penetration into the flowing energy that comprises the seemingly stable object. The halo is the key to the processual structure of matter under the mind's deepest gaze.

There are distinct parallels between Gertrude Stein's aesthetic meditation and religious meditation. Both represent as-

cents into higher or unconventional planes of consciousness
which entail a perceptual isolation from conventional reality.
Secondly, and most fascinating, both utilize exercises to decelerate the speed of consciousness. We defined consciousness
speed earlier as the mental time taken for any phenomenon to
pass in and out of awareness. One of the purposes of the mantra or of chanting in traditional religious meditation is to decelerate the consciousness flow to the degree of dissociation, a
shattering of the conventional consciousness field so the ascent
to a "higher reality" might be ascertained. The essence of
chanting is contained in repetition, for it is through the endless restatement of a single utterance that the subject's isolation from extraneous perceptions of external reality is accomplished. Hours of repetition "drug" the chanter and lead
him into a visionary, suprarational realm of single-minded
contemplation.

Gertrude Stein utilizes her syntax as a mantra, but rather
than leading her initiates into a vision of Brahmin her aim is to
raise the material world about her—the farmlands of Bilignin,
the talk of Picabia and Alice Toklas—to the power of an aesthetic object worthy of contemplation. The poem's technique
compels the reader, in the very neuropsychological act of
reading the text, to enter the meditation. Almost every line of
every stanza contains within it endless possibilities of variant
readings. It is in the act of considering these variant readings
that the reader is compelled to consider, to meditate upon the
changes of the matters spoken upon. If in *Four Saints in Three
Acts* the writer good-naturedly invited us to participate in
verbal circus games, in *Stanzas* we are implored to meditate
upon the possibilities of the material world. This poem is not
about the pluralism of James and Whitehead. It *is* that philosophy embodied in artistic technique. The philosophy "happens"
to the reader. Thus the conventional tension between "fitting"
the philosophical message into the poetic form (a problem evident in Eliot's *Four Quartets* and Pound's *Cantos*) does not
exist. In *Stanzas* form is the natural extension of content: the
vision and the craft used to embody the vision are one.

Concentrating within each line all variant readings slows the reading time dramatically and forces the reader's attention upon single lines and single ideas within a line. Meditation might occur on any of several levels. Miss Stein might lead the reader to contemplate the phonemic play possibilities of the poem, as in Part IV, Stanza II:

> I come back to think everything of one
> One and one
> Or not which they were won
> I won.
> They were called I win I won
> Nor which they call not which one or one
> I won.
> I will be winning I won.
> Nor not which one won for this is one.
> I will not think one and one remember not.
> Not I won I won to win win I won one
> And so they declare or they declare
> To declare I declare I declare I win I won one
> I win in which way they manage they manage to win I won
> In I one won in which I win which I win which won I won
> And so they might come to a stanza three
> One or two or one two or one or two or one
> Or one two three all out but one two three
> One of one two three or three of one two and one.[13]

One of the consequences of reading this stanza is that even the words "won" and "win" begin to appear alien to our eyes, sound strange to our ears. Even the sounds and meanings of words as conventional and semantically one-dimensional as "won" and "win" assume when put through these changes a radiance and interest far beyond their place in the conventional language spectrum. Individual words are raised to the power of plastic objects. They can be pondered and appreciated. They assume a physicality, a weight and density, become building blocks in the century's most individual language/consciousness game.

Objects, as well as words, are raised up for contemplation.
There is the Bilignin landscape and scores of unidentified "hes"
and "shes" that speak out of the maelstrom. But the matter,
the stuff of the poem consists chiefly of the words themselves.
Whatever the poem is about it is clearly about itself and the
compositional trials implicit in its construction. What we wit-
ness in *Stanzas* is the movement of the mind in the act of aesthetic meditation as revealed in the technique of the poem.
Meditation is traditionally a most private affair between the
meditator and the object of his meditation. Gertrude Stein has
been audacious enough to leave for us the "worksheets" from
her meditative sessions so that we might retrace her steps and
enter into her meditations.

The aim of all meditative activity, religious or aesthetic,
whether that of Ramakrishna or of Gertrude Stein, is to direct
the mind toward a greater *clarity* of perception. So there is a
distinct rhythm to meditation. From the stage of repetitive
chanting used to achieve a single-mindedness and an isolation
from conventional vision we ascend to the point where the object of contemplation begins to define itself. All meditation can
be viewed as a process of focusing. Indeed, the eye or lens
metaphor is one of the most common to the mystical, visionary experience. The meditator works his way through levels
of consciousness until the most clear definition of the contem-
plative object comes into focus.

This process of tunneling one's way through until the
greatest moment of perceptual clarity is attained is duplicated
in *Stanzas*. Miss Stein engages in a Promethean struggle with
the entire phonemic and intellectual fabric of language until
she arrives at the objects of her contemplation. Much as a Zen
swordsman "tests" the air about him to find those passages
most conducive to the passage of his sword, so Gertrude Stein
toys with the texture of language to find those areas of maximum ambiguity which might become objects for meditation.

I can think of no other literary work in our history that
so extensively and painstakingly explains the operations of the
author's mind in the process of composition. The poem could

be used as a case study for the psycholinguistic study of how
the mind deals with maximally ambiguous syntactic structures.
But it could be utilized, just as successfully by investigators of
the mystical experience (following in the footsteps of William
James and his *Varieties of Religious Experience*) to explore
the spiritual and linguistic dynamics of the mind in active
meditation. And lest we neglect the most essential feature of
the poem, a delight in words and syntax, try reading any of
these stanzas aloud to children:

STANZA XII

> Stanza ten makes a hen
> Stanza third make a bird
> Stanza white make a dog
> Stanza first make it heard
> That I will not not only go there
> But here[.][14]

from STANZA LXVI

> Well well if they wish to sell
> Who adds well well to a wish to sell
> Who adds well to a wish
> Who adds a wish to well
> We do.
> We do.
> We had been as well
> And we do.[15]

A child's first reader in meditation? Or, finally, a phenomenology of mind in rhyme. These are the facets of Gertrude
Stein's genius in the final major experiment of her literary career. A quarter of a century later *Stanzas* still lies in relative
obscurity, a most singular and foreboding-looking monster in
our literary graveyards. But a monster attracting visitors in recent years.

There is one possible analogy to these *Stanzas* in modern
literature and I would identify it as "the poetry of meditation."

I mean not merely a poetry that speaks of the results of a meditative experience but a poetry that leaves behind the traces of the linguistic grappling implicit in the meditative experience. The most famous poem of this form is Wallace Stevens's:

METAPHORS OF A MAGNIFICO

Twenty men crossing a bridge,
Into a village,
Are twenty men crossing twenty bridges,
Into twenty villages,
Or one man
Crossing a single bridge into a village.

This is old song
That will not declare itself. . . .

Twenty men crossing a bridge,
Into a village,
Are
Twenty men crossing a bridge
Into a village.

That will not declare itself
Yet is as certain as meaning. . . .[16]

The old song will not declare itself. Stevens found himself wrestling with Gertrude Stein's dilemma: how does the mind come to know what it knows through language, how does the mind act linguistically in the meditative state? What is this conceptual fisherman's net, this language, that throws itself into the phenomenological sea to bring back what bounty? How much of the richness of the truly real is fated to escape the linguistic nets? Poets who have followed in the wake of both Stevens and Gertrude Stein—George Oppen, Robert Duncan, John Ashbery—are engaged in the same struggle Miss Stein articulated in *Stanzas:* They are meditating upon the word and word structures that would dare to contain and encompass pluralistic reality. It is premature to speak of the success or failure of their attempts. Besides, much of this type of literary experimentation is greeted with baffled silence rather than with noisy judgment. It is difficult to imagine a reenactment of the Stravinsky Rite of Spring riots. Rarely does the most audacious adventure of the avant-garde artist bring more than a coolly phrased critique in this half of the century. Our outrage is contained in whispers or silence of the same variety that Gertrude Stein heard throughout her writing career. But her exploration of the various consciousness states and their correlatives in language has become our modern literary legacy, our locus for aesthetic success or failure: our meditative foundation.

VII
Documents
and Correspondences:
A Conclusion

Throughout this book I have noted the correspondences or analogies to Gertrude Stein's art in other arts or sciences. In this final chapter I present documents concerning these parallels along with some commentary relating this material to the broader image, developed earlier, of the central aims of Gertrude Stein's art.

During the past year of reading Gertrude Stein, I found myself becoming converted to her vision, caught myself repeating her peculiar phraseology in my own writing or speaking. And most vitally, I have found Miss Stein's thinking on the language/consciousness issue magnetic in its power to draw together knowledge from other disciplines. A mandala of sorts developed with Gertrude Stein at its focal center and with psychology, linguistics, anthropology, communication theory, and the plastic arts as points on its circumference. Some of the ties between Miss Stein and these other areas are indeed tenuous. Others I feel assured defending. There are possibilities opened by Gertrude Stein, particularly in the field of linguistic analysis that could lead in numerous directions. I have chosen several, and in the documents will introduce several more.

These documents represent statements of positions that I felt interacted directly with Miss Stein's chief artistic concerns. They also reflect my own biases toward what is broadly categorized "avant-garde" art. An alternative selection of documents is certainly possible as well as perhaps preferable to some readers. These are merely my own compass points, trail markings that I have found whilst exploring Gertrude Stein's writing. They reflect my own intellectual preferences and prejudices: clinical psychiatry, Whorfian metalinguistics, philosophical phenomenology, radical literary experimentalism. The interaction between these current personal interests and a reading of Gertrude Stein brought about this book and this approach.

So with all the humility and arrogance befitting the task

I present a further development of these parallels, and a record of the evidence that led to the formulation of this study.

One note on the form itself: each document, or group of documents related by a central theme, will be followed by a statement summarizing content of the document and its relation to the corpus of Gertrude Stein's writing.

There is no final word on Gertrude Stein.

That is my intention and I believe it was hers.

THE REVOLUTION OF THE WORD

Document #1

The language of poetry is not in the ordinary sense communicative: but the normal power of reference possessed by words and sentences, their power to point fairly unambiguously at items in the world, is usually taken for granted. Precision of reference had been sometimes more, sometimes less, important to the poet; but now suddenly it seems the whole referential character of language had become for him a sort of irritant or stumbling block. It was as if the poet began to see the world with a dreadful particularity, as a great ineffable mass of inextricable processes. To lose the discursive "thingy" nature of one's vision and yet to feel the necessity of utterance is to experience a breakdown of language—which may be met in two ways. The poet may accept or even intensify his sense of the chaotic interpenetration of reality, and attempt to make his language into the perfect expression of this overrich world. To do this is to weaken the referential character of language by overloading it. On the other hand the poet may attempt to draw language out of the ineffable flux altogether, and to erect it into a pure and non-referential structure on its own.

—*Sartre* by Iris Murdoch[1]

I am drawn to Iris Murdoch's statement on several counts. First, she asserts the fundamental phenomenological reality for an artist like Sartre or Gertrude Stein: that reality is radically

processual, concrete, and hence fragmentary. It is an old statement that has been repeated ad infinitum but it deserves to be
heard once again. The reality the literary artist inherited after
the first World War was literally in pieces. It was as W. B.
Yeats wrote in "The Second Coming": "Things fall apart, the
center cannot hold." The center did not hold. Along with the
physical material damage caused by the war, there was a collapse not only of the old moral, religious, ethical values but
also of the aesthetic. It is a moot question as to whether the
artist anticipates revolutions in his social reality or is a step behind them. It is my own belief that the literary arts in America
and Europe circa 1918 were a step behind.

Given the fragmentary world, this shattered compositional field, of what use is the old referential semantic skeleton
of language? What whole things were there left to refer to?
This is what I find in Iris Murdoch's statement, and it fuses in
my mind with Gertrude Stein's essay "Composition as Explanation." Their point is identical, although Iris Murdoch gives
the broader picture. In response to fragmentary reality the
writer can overload his words as well as not load them—Rimbaud versus Mallarmé. Or, to my mind, Joyce, particularly of
Finnegans Wake, versus Gertrude Stein. The phrase "to see
the world with a dreadful particularity" seems to me to be
more relevant to Sartre or to the schizophrenic experience than
to Gertrude Stein—who shared with her teacher William
James the delight of the paticularity of matter.

Document #2

To make a dadaist poem
Take a newspaper.
Take a pair of scissors.
Choose an article as long as you are planning to make
your poem
Cut out the article.
Then cut out each of the words that make up this
article & put them in a bag.

Shake it gently.
Then take out the scraps one after another in the order
in which they left the bag.
Copy conscientiously.
The poem will be like you.

—Tristan Tzara, *Dadaist Manifesto*[2]

If Europe after World War I resembled a bottomless garbage
pail Tristan Tzara and his friends reminded us that the contents of the pail were indeed garbage. They exulted in the
universal disorder, sang over the ruins. I feel that the essence
of Tzara's song was mockery. In a wholly illogical world why
retain any logic in language? Lurking behind this premise is
the foreboding question: why have art? Why have literature
at all? Hence the poem out of the paper bag which could just
as well be the product of a lunatic or an infant as of Tzara
himself. The words out of the bag correspond to the social
reality. Only chance beauty, the beauty of one piece of rubble
accidentally tumbling on top of another seems to count for
Tzara. Verbal beauty also seems to be the product of chance,
without logic, without a prior design.

I feel the connection between Tzara's dadaism and Gertrude Stein's work tenuous but worth considering. They are
both attacking the old ways of literary language but from totally different positions with radically different ends in mind.
Gertrude Stein was never a dadaist in program or spirit. She
knew of them, and knew Tzara personally but went her own
way. My feeling is that she did not feel the brunt of the collapse of Western civilization after the war, as did Tzara. She
gives me the impression of simply not knowing what was going
on. After all, she had always lived a sheltered, upper-middle
class life apart from the harsher social realities of war and
poverty. Her attack on the old literary language was intellectual, disinterested, and grew out of her classes with William
James. Her sundering of conventional English syntax was a
rational, conscious response to a laboratory problem: how can
consciousness be altered by unconventional word patterning.

On the other hand, Tzara's "laboratory" was the world he inhabited and his assault on conventional syntax was part of a larger program of absolute nihilism, passionately and irrationally declared. Tzara and Gertrude Stein share only one similarity: they attempt to bridge the gulf between what they see as twentieth-century reality and the language and compositional procedures of the writer in his attempts to describe it. The comparisons of Tzara and Miss Stein are also useful to answer Miss Stein's critics (including B. F. Skinner) who accuse her of chance or automatic writing.

Document #3

TIRED OF THE SPECTACLE OF SHORT STORIES, NOVELS, POEMS AND PLAYS STILL UNDER THE HEGEMONY OF THE BANAL WORD, MONOTONOUS SYNTAX, STATIC PSYCHOLOGY, DESCRIPTIVE NATURALISM, AND DESIROUS OF CRYSTALIZING A VIEWPOINT . . .

WE HERE DECLARE THAT:

1. THE REVOLUTION IN THE ENGLISH LANGUAGE IS AN ACCOMPLISHED FACT
2. THE IMAGINATION IN SEARCH OF A FABULOUS WORLD IS AUTONOMOUS AND UNCONFINED
3. PURE POETRY IS A LYRICAL ABSOLUTE THAT SEEKS AN A PRIORI REALITY WITHIN OURSELVES ALONE
4. NARRATIVE IS NOT MERE ANECDOTE, BUT THE PROJECTION OF A METAMORPHOSIS OF REALITY
5. THE EXPRESSION OF THESE CONCEPTS CAN BE ACHIEVED ONLY THROUGH THE RHYTHMIC "HALLUCINATION OF THE WORD" (Rimbaud)
6. THE LITERARY CREATOR HAS THE RIGHT TO DISINTEGRATE THE PRIMAL MATTER OF WORDS IMPOSED ON HIM BY TEXTBOOKS AND DICTIONARIES
7. HE HAS THE RIGHT TO USE WORDS OF HIS OWN

FASHIONING AND TO DISREGARD EXISTING
GRAMMATICAL AND SYNTACTICAL LAWS
8. THE "LITANY OF WORDS" IS ADMITTED AS AN IN-
   DEPENDENT UNIT
9. WE ARE NOT CONCERNED WITH THE PROPAGA-
   TION OF SOCIAL IDEAS . . .
10. TIME IS A TYRANNY TO BE ABOLISHED
11. THE WRITER EXPRESSES. HE DOES NOT COMMU-
    NICATE
12. THE PLAIN READER BE DAMNED.[3]

—Eugene Jolas[3]

I have included Jolas's manifesto to indicate how widespread
the complaints against the old literary language were among
American writers. Jolas used this manifesto for his own reasons—he was an orthodox surrealist for a time, then broke away
from André Breton to form his own brand of surrealism—but
its value still remains as a document of moods circa 1927. Jolas
edited *transition*, a magazine that published a very broad spectrum of the avant-garde from the surrealists to James Joyce
and Gertrude Stein. In this manifesto, which reads more like
an editorial statement than an esthetic one, Jolas attempts to
synthesize the findings of some dozen schools of writing (cubism, futurism, surrealism) and sculpt them into the base of his
own surrealism—which was more mystically and Jungian ori-
ented than that of André Breton.

Forgetting Jolas's own synthesis, the manifesto says much
for a linguistic metamorphosis that closely parallels Stein.
NARRATIVE IS NOT MERE ANECDOTE, BUT THE
PROJECTION OF A METAMORPHOSIS OF REALITY"
strikes me as the crux of the matter in *Three Lives* and *The
Making of Americans*. The narrative in Gertrude Stein cap-
tures the changes of the real world; it reads awkwardly, since
reality changes awkwardly. The points about the right of the
writer to shape his own language hardly need repeating here.
What is most astute is Jolas's THE "LITANY OF WORDS"
IS ADMITTED AS AN INDEPENDENT UNIT. Before writ-
ing about *Tender Buttons* I made several tapes of myself read-

ing the book and played them ad infinitum until I had a feeling
for the rhythms of the various sections. The first forms they
resembled for me were litanies, incantations, prayers, chants:
the endless, repeating phrases, the feeling of insistence in lines
without apparent sense, the refrains.

Document #4

One of the most interesting facts about the Chinese language is
that in it you can see, not only the forms of sentences, but literally
the parts of speech growing up, budding forth one from another.
Like nature, the Chinese words are alive and plastic, because thing
and action are not separated.

—Fenollosa, *The Chinese Written
Character As A Medium for Poetry*[4]

Whether or not Fenollosa's interpretation of the role of the
Chinese ideograph is correct, the point that the beauty of the
Chinese language resides in its capacity to be processual (and
hence duplicate the operations of nature) is well taken.

My first contact with Fenollosa's theory applied to English was in Pound. In the *A.B.C. of Reading*, but more specifically for me in the *Cantos*, Pound seemed to canonize Fenollosa's complaint against the staticity and abstractness of conventional English syntax and insisted that young poets deal
with the material in front of their noses: the concrete, immediate, and processual.

I have connected Fenollosa with Gertrude Stein because
of Fenollosa's premise that the more plastic and nature-
grounded the language the poet uses the more moving is his
artistic success. When Miss Stein speaks of the necessity of
writing to "go on" she seems to be narrowing the gap between
life and art, artistic perception and everyday perception. Because the nature of the world is that it is always "going on,"
because the mind of the artist is also continuously in motion,
should not the English-language writer find some word organization which will capture this motion with as much verisi-
militude as possible?

THE LINGUISTIC RELATIVITY THESIS

Document #5

Human beings do not live in the objective world alone, not alone in the world of social activity as ordinarily understood but are very much at the mercy of the particular language which has become the medium for expression in their society. The fact of the matter is that the "real world" is to a large extent unconsciously built up on the language habits of the group. . . . We see and hear and otherwise experience very largely as we do because the language habits of our community predispose certain choices of interpretation.

—Edward Sapir[5]

The linguistic/relativity thesis of Sapir and Whorf was my starting point for this project. If Whorf is correct and our language determines our reality sense, might not a new language, like Gertrude Stein's, open the possibility of entering another, an alternative reality?

And if Miss Stein leads us to a different reality is it the same process-oriented universe of the Hopi Indian that Whorf explicated?

These questions are still open for me. The attractiveness of matching Whorf with Gertrude Stein is undercut by the inconclusiveness of research that has followed in Whorf's footsteps. The Whorfian hypothesis is just that: a hypothesis. But its relevance to the literary revolution is something I feel certain of. No matter that neither Eugene Jolas nor Gertrude Stein had the faintest notion of who Whorf was. Their attempts to go beyond the perceptual boundaries established by conventional language usage represent a strong analog to the Whorfian thesis.

I see Gertrude Stein as a visionary writer. It is not her "message," whatever there is of it, that I find visionary, how-

ever. It is her raising of the powers of language into the
spheres of word mysticism, her resurrection of tea-room language into something more abstract, something less bound by
the shopworn habits of our linguistic community. Her language moves us from the world of commonplaceness into a
realm beyond: the beauty of buttons and oranges in *Tender
Buttons*, the saints of *Four Saints*, the earth, sky, and moun-
tains of *The World Is Round*. In Gertrude Stein's work we
find the theories Whorf applied with the mind of a psychologist and the fancifulness of a clown or a poet.

NEURO-PHYSIOLOGICAL CORRELATIVES
TO EXPERIMENTAL WORD PATTERNING

Document #6

The first process of education is obviously not a mental process.
When a mother talks to a baby, she is not encouraging its little
mind to think. When she is coaxing her child to walk, she is not
making a theoretical exposition of the science of equilibration. She
crouches before the child, at a little distance, and spreads her
hands, "Come, baby—come to mother. Come! Baby, walk! Yes,
walk! Come along. A little walk to its mother. Come! Come then!
Why, yes, what a pretty baby! . . . No, don't be frightened, dear.
No—Come to mother—" and she catches the little pinafore by the
tip—and the infant lurches forward. "There! There! A beautiful
walk. . . ."

Now who will tell me that this talk has any rhyme or reason?
Not a spark of reason. Yet a real rhyme, or rhythm, much more
important. The song and the urge of the mother's voice plays directly on the affective centers of the child, a wonderful stimulus
and intuition. The words hardly matter. . . .

—D. H. Lawrence, *Fantasia of the Unconscious*[6]

What led me to Gertrude Stein was an interest in powers of
language other than the semantic. The excitement of reading

her work for the first time was heightened by the discovery of a number of language powers long neglected by writers who had considered the semantic weight of words primary and all their coloristic or psycho-neurological powers secondary. Why do words tire us—make us laugh or moan, sexually entice us or desensitize us—apart from the actual referential meaning they hold?

The Lawrence quote is relevant because it reminds us that a child is sensitive to the sound patterns of words even before he attains semantic awareness. What I understand of Piaget, Church, *et al.* seems to affirm Lawrence's premise. The rhythm and play of words, which Lawrence hints might closely parallel the rhythms of bodily processes themselves, can communicate just as effectively as semantic communications. Just how this process occurs I cannot say. I have researched this area of language rhythm and physiological rhythm fully and have found extremely little literature on the subject, although there is an enormous literature on verbal learning focusing on the acquisition of semantic sense.

This is a peculiar state of affairs considering how greatly the psychoanalytic scheme depends upon word powers and patternings to effect a cure. In psychotherapy a patient is literally talked well, and the manner in which the talk is articulated is just as vital as the semantic content of it. I have attended therapy sessions in which the analyst intentionally created verbal puzzles in order to communicate attitudes not possible in conventional linear statements. The situation is reminiscent of the Zen master's use of Koan in instructing a religious initiate.

I'm reminded of Robert Kelly's statement concerning the necessity of creating new verbal structures that *are* something, rather than stand for something. Consider this lullaby by Gertrude Stein:

A LESSON FOR BABY

What is milk. Milk is a mouth. What is a mouth.
Sweet. What is sweet. Baby.

A lesson for baby.
What is a mixture. Good all the time.
Who is good all the time. I wonder.
A lesson for baby.
What is a melon. A little round.
Who is a little round. Baby.[7]

The repetitions, in lines, the consonantal plays between words, the rhythms all serve to soothe, to induce relaxation. I would like to see the poem above repeated to infants as a lullaby. I think it would meet with as much if not more success than any of the conventional formulas. This poem is not about sleep, it is a falling off to sleep and the key is its patterning. "Milk" can be replaced by "moon"; but the power of the sounds organized to form something other than a conventional everyday music remains.

THE WORD AS DRUG

Document #7

The song constitutes a purely psychological treatment, for the shaman does not touch the body of the sick woman and administers no remedy. Nevertheless it involves, directly and explicitly, the pathological condition and its locus. In our view the song constitutes a psychological manipulation of the sick organ, and it is precisely from this manipulation that a cure is expected. . . .

The shaman provides the sick woman with a language by means of which unexpressed, and otherwise inexpressible, psychic states can be immediately expressed. And it is this transition to verbal expression—at the same time making it possible to undergo in an ordered and intelligible form a real experience that would otherwise be chaotic and inexpressible—which induces the release of the psychological process, that is, the reorganization in a favorable direction, of the process to which the sick woman is subjected.

—Claude Lévi-Strauss, *Structural Anthropology*[8]

The Lévi-Strauss statement on word power and shamanism above reminds us that the song made sacred by society acts psysiologically on the body, and can provide a roadway for otherwise inexpressible feelings (strong shades of Whorf!). The unusual word pattern might open gateways into the emotional self otherwise blocked by conventionalized language and conventionalized living.

SOME FINAL REMARKS ON LANGUAGE AND BODY CONSCIOUSNESS

Document #8

The Human Being are strung lines of word associates that control "thoughts feelings and *apparent* sensory impressions." Quote from Encephalographic Research Chicago Written in TIME. See Page 156 Naked Lunch Burroughs. See and hear what They expect to see and hear because The Word Lines keep Thee in Slots.

Cut the Word Lines with scissors or switch blade as preferred. The Word Lines keep you in Time. . . . Cut the in lines. . . . Make out lines to Space. Take a page of your own writing of you write or a letter or a newspaper article or a page or less or more of any writer living or dead. . . . Cut into sections. Down the middle. And cross the sides. . . . Rearrange the sections. . . . Write the result message. . . .

—William Burroughs and Brion Gysin, *The Exterminator*[9]

The discrepancy between time and sensation as experienced in the body and as described in our conventional language uses is explored here. The tie between Burroughs and Gertrude Stein is a strong one. Burroughs was introduced to Gertrude Stein's writing as an undergraduate at Harvard majoring in linguistic anthropology. At Harvard he also met a collagist—Brion Gysin, who was a friend of Alice B. Toklas and who gave Miss Toklas her notorious hashish brownie recipe. My own

acquaintance with Burroughs's writing came about by finding his book *The Exterminator* at the time I was first reading
Whorf. Burroughs's idea of cutting into the habitual word
lines so as to enable the reader to enter another consciousness
dimension (an idea found in its most advanced form in Burroughs's most recent book *The Ticket That Exploded*) resembles Whorf's ideas applied to communication theory. It
also strikes me as an extension of a way of reading Gertrude
Stein that I have suggested in this study.

Document #9

What is the grammar of pain?

—Wittgenstein

Suppose I want to keep a diary of the recurrence of a certain sensation. To this end I associate it with the sign E and write this sign
down every time I experience this sensation. Imagine a person with
a memory so bad he is always forgetting what the word "pain"
means and keeps calling different things by that name: "I believe
this is E again."

—Wittgenstein, *Philosophical Investigations*[10]

Wittgenstein comes to mind as a grandfather figure standing
behind writers such as Burroughs and as a father figure to his
contemporaries, including Gertrude Stein. As far as I can de-
termine, Gertrude Stein knew nothing directly of Wittgenstein's philosophy. She did know, however, something of Alfred
Whitehead's work with Wittgensteinian problems. The importance of Wittgenstein's philosophy to the cause of literary
modernism cannot be underestimated. While Eugene Jolas declared the artistic necessity of breaking through the syntax of
the old literary language, Wittgenstein established the philosophical imperative to break through the conventional language
barriers. Wittgenstein seems to reduce the discipline of philosophy to a linguistic dilemma. Philosophy, he seems to say, is
preposterous and nonsensical because it must depend upon

framing its propositions in a language that is utterly nonsensical and illogical in terms of its grounding in objective reality. Hence, words and grammatical patternings are merely more of man's conceptual lattices, constructed to explain an unexplainable objective reality.

The writing of Gertrude Stein can be seen as a consequence of the Wittgensteinian attack on the referential connection between language and what is truly "out-there."

INTENSIFIED VISUAL PERCEPTION AND LINGUISTIC REPORT

Document #10

From an experience under psilocybin:

"Doctor," I say, "where've you been? I'm Alabama bound, I'm carbamino bound, I love to bound, to move about, and to play the violin, olin, playing the violinnnnnnnn . . . ohhhhhh HI diddle dee-dee, a spinach life for me. Garumph, Doctor, Garumph. Ahem. Hey Doc, listen: ABCDEFGHIJKLMNOP. QRS and TUV, W, and XYZ. . . ."[11]

—Daniel Breslaw, *The Drug Experience*[11]

Document #11

From a psychopathic episode of an institutionized mental patient undergoing visual hallucination:

(In response to the inquiry: "How do you feel about God?") Boy, we do. He is love himself, he measures one hundred and thirty two per cent on Love that is higher than anyone else in Heaven or on Earth except Jesus Christ who is one hundred and fifty six and as I mentioned you know the Father is all Love and compassion . . . he is the most honored boy in the whole big earth today and is so modest he won't even think about it.

—Harry Sullivan,
Schizophrenia as Human Process[12]

I am considering the drug experience and the psychopathic episode here solely in terms of visual report. Whether the psilocybin creates an artificial, short-lived psychosis identical to the psychopathic state is a question I cannot begin to answer. I can, however, note the following similarities in the two experiences in terms of their verbal reports. In both states, conventionalized perceptions of temporal and spatial boundaries collapse. In both states, the consciousness field is widened to include the simultaneous perception of a variety of things not immediately perceptible to someone in conventional consciousness.

What all this heightened visual perception implies linguistically is the total breakdown of conventional word patterning. The broadening of the visual field, the heightening of visual sensitivity brings about the collapse of the conventional, English sentence structure which implies a one-item-at-a-time logical categorization of visual perception. In everyday consciousness we attend, unhurriedly, to one item at a time. Now I see a chair, now I see a table, and so on. Under psilocybin or in a psychopathic episode, the perceptual field is too full to be compressed into a standard subject-verb-object matrix.

Several years ago I participated in an experiment involving mescaline and the creative process. During the first hour under the drug I found my visual field so filled with objects, so saturated with things, that the very idea of capturing it on paper seemed futile, and I stopped after two pages.

How does all of this apply to Gertrude Stein, who never suffered a psychopathic episode or tasted any drug more potent than Alice Toklas's hashish brownies?

One of the claims I have made for Gertrude Stein's writing is that it has the possibility of altering the reader's consciousness. The problem can be approached from the other side. What are the characteristics of the verbal reports of those undergoing an unconventional consciousness state? What similarities exist between the mind under drug influence speaking and the speaking mind drugging itself? Why, when a speaker drops the semantic covers of his words, do they tend to fall

into certain phonemic or morphemic sequences? The consonantal play in the drug report ("I'm carbamino bound, I love
to bound/violin/olin") is also central to Gertrude Stein's
Tender Buttons. But in Gertrude Stein the intention is mani-
fested in conscious art. Are there intrinsic characteristics of
the mind that will group sound sequences regardless of semantic considerations? If so, what are the consequences for
literary theory as well as for psychology? These are questions
brought to my mind by such a comparison. Not whether evidence can be found as to whether Gertrude Stein was "mad,"
but why her verbal "madness" is part of our psychological
and cultural history and reality.

INTENSIFIED ACOUSTICAL PERCEPTION
AND THE AMERICAN LANGUAGE

Document #12

The Twenties accepted the dominance of the ear of song and
dance, over literacy and civilization. Even the high brow arts of
the Twenties were "jung and easily Freudened" and moved en-
thusiastically toward the retribalization of society. The famous
family of Stein (Gert and Ep and Ein) presents a good cross-sec-
tion of the new tribalism of the new (radio) environment.

—Marshall McLuhan,
The Reversal of the Overheated Image.[13]

All the documents prior to Number 10 have considered language abstractly, language as a system grounded in Aristotelian
logic and its consequences on thought. I would now like to
consider American English specifically and the various techniques used by Gertrude Stein to alter it. Kenneth Rexroth
once suggested that Stein played with tendencies latent in
American English. The full impact of Rexroth's statement did
not strike me until I found further support for it in Marshall
McLuhan's writings.

I have borrowed from McLuhan when convenient and discarded when necessary. McLuhan in the selection above hammers at his "medium-is-the-massage" message. The creation of the radio medium he sees as bringing about a variety of cultural changes. Foremost among these is the heightening of the individual's acoustical sense. I agree with McLuhan (although the argument is probably scientifically unprovable) and would apply it in this manner.

The radio does intensify our awareness of certain characteristics latent in American speech. I have taped and studied late evening disc-jockey programs on a variety of stations and found that nearly all of these performers speak a peculiar variety of our language. Their vocabulary is vastly simplified. They speak a variety of basic English, the only unconventional words being slang terms. Their message, which is aimed at the greatest possible number of listeners, utilizes a minimal vocabulary. Syntactic intricacy is also minimal, except for a few trick devices. Primary among these devices is repetition. Other devices include simplistic rhymes, consonantal discordance, unconventional pitch shift, and run-on statements.

All of these characteristics are most evident in popular American radio music and in radio advertising. The lyrics of an extremely popular song that filled the radio waves last year utilized the simplest form of repetition. The word inversion of the last line was probably used to save the listener from abject boredom. Whatever the artistic worth of the lyrics the repetitions got the point of the song across. No one short of idiocy could fail to get the message. Of course all popular music depends on repetition. But music that depends heavily on being heard through radio can be heard only once or twice through the program. The playback possibilities offered in the 1950s and 1960s by the phonograph and tape recorder were not available in the 1920s and 1930s.

As our music endlessly repeats its messages over radio so do our advertisers. Before the techniques of subliminal advertising introduced some measure of subtlety, radio advertisements literally verbally assaulted the listener with imperatives:

BUY! BUY! HURRY! RUSH TO YOUR X STORE! THE SALE ENDS TOMORROW! and so on. The repetitions are molded into a litany. If you can ignore the content, listen to an early morning, ruthlessly evangelical Sunday morning church program and then turn the radio dial until you hear a big city department-store advertisement. They strike the ear as identical: the long, sonorous cadences, the refrains, the rhythms mounting into a grand finale.

I am not suggesting some preposterous theory such as "Americans have a greater proclivity toward repetition than any other people." Beggars in Benares use as much repetition to get their alms as any Madison Avenue huckster. I am suggesting, however, that the radio medium has exaggerated and redefined our sensibilities toward certain characteristics of our daily language usage. I think McLuhan's link between Gertrude Stein and the radio environment is astute and deserves further research and speculation.

EXAMPLES OF POST-STEINIAN LITERATURE

Document #13

woodpecker
            grabber
woodpecker
            nice
woodpecker
            stone
woodpecker
            flask
woodpecker
            un
woodpecker
            reader
woodpecker
            guard

woodpecker
        plunger
woodpecker
        staple
woodpecker
        gravel
woodpecker
        grape
woodpecker
        taper
woodpecker
        card
woodpecker
        crepe
woodpecker
        cup
woodpecker
        glove
woodpecker
        slag
woodpecker
        clock
woodpecker
        smudge
woodpecker
        coffee

—Clark Coolidge[14]

As Stein has most clearly & accurately indicated, words have a universe of qualities other than descriptive relation: Hardness, Density, SoundShape, vector-force, & degree of Transparency/ Opacity. I am attempting to peer through the lines into this possible Word Art Landscape, work within it & return with Word-scapes, Word objects to refresh the mind so currently overloaded with centuries of medial language-tape.

—Clark Coolidge[15]

Clark Coolidge, a young West Coast poet strongly influenced by Gertrude Stein summarizes the point of view I have

adopted in this book. The old literary criticisms simply do not have categories for phenomena such as "word density," or "utterance speed," or "word object transparency." I have offered a few categories in this book (speed, continuity, density, linguistic moment) in an attempt to describe what I, together with Clark Coolidge, feel to be the foundation of Gertrude Stein's writing.

Document #14

—from *Copyright 1968 by Aram Saroyan*
by Aram Saroyan, Kulchur Press, New York, 1968.[16]

The material found on this and the previous page is a poem from Saroyan's volume.

Document #15

Shakespeare Milton
Shakespeare Milton

Shelley as well
Shelley as well

Sarah something Teasdale
Sarah something Teasdale

Edith M. Bell
Edith M. Bell

—Lewis Welch, from *On Oct.*[17]

This is a humorous interlude from a longer poem by Lewis Welch who wrote his Senior Thesis at Reed College on Gertrude Stein and occasionally uses her stylisms in his own poems. More serious applications of Miss Stein's techniques in the work of contemporary poets follow:

Document #16

(TENSORS) #2

> in the in between they are
> under this & only this
>
> this is their that, & all
> their together with it,
> is next to it, next to it
> & then inside.
>
> all of it, she said.
> all of this, he said.
>
> they said their who
> to each other, & their
> this, their this
> is even ever again &
> now
>
>> who is this.
>> who is this.
>> he said.
>> she said.
>> this is who.

—Robert Kelly, from *Finding the Measure*[18]

Robert Kelly's poem seems to apply Gertrude Stein's principles more stringently than Miss Stein did herself. Given an absolute, limited vocabulary (pronouns, prepositions, conjunctions) what can the poet do to their patterning to establish a communication? Volumes of Gertrude Stein consist of nothing more than the workings out of the patterning possibilities of limited—and, like Kelly's, nounless—vocabularies.

Document #17

A RATTLE FOR BABY I

> Who rattles in sleep. Sleep rattles. Where rattles are.
> A tongue. Who rattles in sleep. Sleep.

& persuades us.
Where tongues are. Everyone tastes us.
The longer we taste. He awaits us.
& persuades us.
Where cinnamons are. In his mouth.
& his mouth rattles it. Matthew.

—Jerome Rothenberg[19]

Responses to Gertrude Stein from contemporary American poets have ranged from conscious imitation (Jerome Rothenberg, Robert Duncan, Clark Coolidge) to free recreations only slightly grounded in Miss Stein's styles. The above, for example, is Jerome Rothenberg's close imitation of a before-quoted Gertrude Stein piece *Lesson for Baby*.

Document #18

NOTE: Each line . . . of these poems is regulated for expressive purposes, as to speed of delivery, loudness, and duration of silence following it. Speeds include very very slowly (VVS), very slowly (VS), slowly (S), moderately slowly (MS), moderately (M), moderately rapidly (MR), rapidly (R), very rapidly (VR), and very very rapidly (VVR). Degrees of loudness include softly (P), moderately softly (MP), moderately loudly (MF), loudly (F), and very loudly (FF). Durations of silence are given in seconds. . . .

mr/mp   I have started again to write poems that say things to
              people   1
r/mf   I even write a chance poem that says & says & says   ½
vr/mf   Tho I let chance order the words and structure them
              as I've usually done for the last five years   3

—Jackson McLow, *Friendship Poems*[20]

The above, on the other hand, is a radical reworking of Gertrude Stein's techniques, written by Jackson McLow.

And, finally, a last comment:

Document #19

I see a snake like beauty in the living changes of syntax.

—Robert Duncan,
from *The Opening of the Field*[21]

VIII
Postscript

It would be most convenient for me to end this book with a concluding statement indicating why Gertrude Stein and Wittgenstein and Sullivan and McLuhan are all comrades in the modernist revolution of the word. It would be as easy as it would be dishonest. The documents represent points of discovery for me, not easily accepted, exact correspondences, and I offer them in this spirit. I see them as points for future take-offs in Steinian research. There are at present only three full-length critical studies of Gertrude Stein's compositional methods, and all fail to consider much of the material in this book—which itself discusses only a fraction of Miss Stein's work. Seven volumes of the eight-volume Yale University series have never received critical illumination. There is much work to be done, and I hope this book represents a step in the direction of further research.

In *Art by Subtraction: A Dissenting Opinion of Gertrude Stein*, B. L. Reid boldly declares that Gertrude Stein's contribution to twentieth-century literature is nil, that she had impact on no other artists save a few cranks, and that she will be forgotten entirely in a decade or so.

If I have succeeded in accomplishing anything in this book, I hope it has been the establishment of the importance of Gertrude Stein's art to the entire modern literary movement, and an indication of the possibilities opened to artists who followed in her footsteps. My own feeling toward her work is as broadly sympathetic as Reid's is antagonistic. But regardless of my or Mr. Reid's opinions the fact remains that Miss Stein followed a program essential to modern literature. John Malcolm Brinnin suggests that if Gertrude Stein had not lived and written in the manner in which she did, someone else would have had to.

Her appeal has always been select. Writers and painters seem as a group most responsive to her experimentation. Perhaps her influence has been most acute on modern poets, since

poets are continually being absorbed by language and intoxi-
cated by the effects it can evoke. There is a music, a power in
Gertrude Stein's work at which I have only hinted in this
book. William Carlos Williams likens her words to crowds at
Coney Island as seen from a plane at high altitude. The Coney
Island comparison invokes a sense of fun and riotous beauty
that I find central in Miss Stein's work.

Her appeal might be first to artists, but Carl Van Vechten
reports leaving the Chicago Opera house hearing children in the
corridors shout: "Pigeons on the grass alas. Pigeons on the
grass alas."

If I have asked you to consider Gertrude Stein's connection with all the various literary and psychological schools of
this century, with all the technological innovations and philosophical revolutions, I would ask you, finally, to consider the
language of her art as a magic, a power recorded in the children's refrain: sense and nonsense, art and living, intellect and
heart.

Notes

Chapter I: Introduction

1. Samuel Beckett, and Sixteen Other Authors, *Our Exagmination Round His Factification for Incamination of Work in Progress*, p. 77
2. Gertrude Stein, *Portraits and Prayers*, p. 121
3. Maurice Nadeau, *The History of Surrealism*. See also André Breton, *Manifesto of Surrealism*
4. Edmund Wilson, *Axel's Castle*, p. 284
5. Robert Kelly and Paris Leary, eds., *A Controversy of Poets*, p. 564
6. Walker Gibson, ed., *The Limits of Language*, p. 8
7. Kenneth Rexroth, *Bird in the Bush*, p. 10
8. Edmund Wilson, *Axel's Castle*, p. 296

Chapter II: "Melanctha"

1. Gertrude Stein, *Lectures in America*, p. 138
2. William James, *The Principles of Psychology*, vol. 1, p. 121

3. W. E. B. Lewis, *The American Adam*
4. Gertrude Stein, *Lectures in America*, p. 137
5. Donald Sutherland, *Gertrude Stein: A Biography of Her Work*, p. 10
6. *Ibid.*, p. 11
7. Gertrude Stein, *Selected Writings*, p. 517
8. *Ibid.*, p. 137
9. Gertrude Stein, *Three Lives*, p. 85
10. *Ibid.*, p. 122
11. Gertrude Stein, *Three Lives*, p. 122
12. Gertrude Stein, *Lectures in America*, p. 176
13. *Three Lives*, p. 138
14. *Ibid.*, p. 139
15. Gertrude Stein, *Lectures in America*, p. 138
16. Gertrude Stein, *Three Lives*, p. 149
17. John Malcolm Brinnin, *The Third Rose: Gertrude Stein and Her World*, p. 35

Chapter III: The Making of Americans

1. Leon Katz, from an unpublished doctoral dissertation, "The First *Making of Americans*," p. 24
2. Gertrude Stein, *The Making of Americans*, p. 3
3. Gertrude Stein, *Lectures in America*, p. 140
4. Gertrude Stein, *The Making of Americans*, p. 7
5. *Ibid.*, p. 303
6. Gertrude Stein, *Selected Writings*, pp. 513, 518
7. Gertrude Stein, *The Making of Americans*, p. 190
8. *Ibid.*, p. 177
9. *Ibid.*, p. 456
10. *Ibid.*, p. 31
11. *Ibid.*, p. 28
12. *Ibid.*, p. 10
13. Michael Hoffman, *The Development of Abstractionism in the Writings of Gertrude Stein*, p. 99
14. Gertrude Stein, *The Making of Americans*, p. 388
15. *Ibid.*, p. 34
16. *Ibid.*, p. 38

17. Gertrude Stein, *Lectures in America*, p. 138
18. *Ibid.*, p. 147
19. *Ibid.*, p. 193
20. *Ibid.*, p. 217
21. Gertrude Stein, *The Making of Americans*, p. 915
22. Maurice Marleau-Ponty, "Cézanne's Doubt," *Art and Literature*, 23, pp. 106-14

Chapter IV: Tender Buttons

1. Quoted in Norman Brown, *Life Against Death*, p. 71
2. Gertrude Stein, *Lectures in America*, p. 238
3. R. D. Laing, *The Politics of Experience*, p. 100
4. Lewis Carroll, *Alice's Adventures in Wonderland*
5. Joseph Church, *Language and the Discovery of Reality*, p. 77
6. See William Wells Newell, *Games and Songs of American Children* for these and other traditional word games
7. *Ibid.*, p. 201
8. Irving Lee, ed., *The Language of Wisdom and Folly*, p. 241
9. *Ibid.*, p. 242
10. Claude Lévi-Strauss, *Structural Anthropology*, p. 196
11. Sherwood Anderson, introduction to Gertrude Stein, *Geography and Plays*, p. 7
12. Gertrude Stein, *Selected Writings*, p. 461
13. B. F. Skinner, "Has Gertrude Stein a Secret?" *Atlantic*, January 1934, pp. 53-57
14. Gertrude Stein, *Lectures in America*, p. 191
15. Michael Hoffman, *The Development of Abstractionism in The Writings of Gertrude Stein*, p. 202
16. Gertrude Stein, *Selected Writings*, p. 491
17. Gertrude Stein, *Lectures in America*, p. 242
18. Gertrude Stein, *Selected Writings*, p. 495
19. *Ibid.*, p. 492
20. See Arthur and Leonora Hornblow's *Animals Do the Strangest Things* for more examples of this form of children's definition.
21. William Carlos Williams, *Selected Essays*, p. 163
22. *Ibid.*, p. 164

Chapter V: Four Saints in Three Acts

1. Kenneth Burke, in John Malcolm Brinnin, *The Third Rose*, p. 326
2. Gertrude Stein, *Selected Writings*, p. 612
3. Gertrude Stein, *Lectures in America*, p. 112
4. For further details concerning the Virgil Thomson/Gertrude Stein collaboration on *Four Saints*, see *Virgil Thomson* by Virgil Thomson (Knopf, 1962) and the liner notes to the recording of *Four Saints in Three Acts* (RCA, LM-2756)
5. Gertrude Stein, *Selected Writings*, p. 581
6. *Ibid.*, p. 585
7. Gertrude Stein, *As Fine as Melanctha*, p. 197
8. Gertrude Stein, *Selected Writings*, p. 534–35
9. *Ibid.*, p. 607
10. Gertrude Stein, *Lectures in America*, p. 129
11. Donald Sutherland, *Gertrude Stein: A Biography*, p. 123
12. Gertrude Stein, *Selected Writings*, p. 586
13. *Ibid.*, p. 585
14. *Ibid.*, p. 598
15. *Ibid.*, p. 583
16. *Ibid.*, p. 594
17. *Ibid.*, p. 595
18. *Ibid.*, pp. 600–01
19. *Ibid.*, p. 604
20. Gertrude Stein, *Lectures in America*, p. 95
21. Examples of Miss Stein's impact on contemporary theater cannot only be found among the "Theater of the Absurd" playwrights such as Beckett, Ionesco, Arrabel, and Pinter but also among the "underground" playwrights of the 1950s and 1960s. Most interesting in this regard is the drama of Ruth Krauss collected in *There's a little ambiguity over there among the bluebells* (Something Else Press, 1968) and the plays in *The New Underground Theatre*, edited by Robert Schroeder (Bantam Books, 1968). The notion of the play as landscape was explored in depth by the "happening" movement centered in New York City in the late 1950s. Worthy of note are the happenings of Jackson MacLow, Dick Hig-

gins, Al Hansen, and Alison Knowle. Some striking parallels between the dramatic "happening" and primitive ritual are drawn in Jerome Rothenberg's *Technicians of the Sacred.* See pp. 107–28, 449–50

22. Gertrude Stein, *Selected Writings*, pp. 514–15

Chapter VI: Stanzas in Meditation

1. William James, *A Pluralistic Universe*, p. 89
2. Gertrude Stein, *Selected Writings*, p. 487
3. Gertrude Stein, *Stanzas in Meditation*, p. 5
4. Quoted in Elizabeth Sprigge, *Gertrude Stein, Her Life and Work*, p. 208
5. Gertrude Stein, *Stanzas in Meditation*, p. 19
6. Gertrude Stein, *Selected Writings*, p. 198
7. Allegra Steward, *Gertrude Stein and the Present*, p. 59
8. Gertrude Stein, *Stanzas in Meditation* p. 67
9. Allegra Steward, *Gertrude Stein and the Present*, p. 61
10. Thornton Wilde in the Foreword to Gertrude Stein, *Four in America*, p. xiii
11. Gertrude Stein, *Lectures in America*, p. 185
12. Gertrude Stein, *Stanzas in Meditation*, p. 102
13. *Ibid.*, p. 68
14. *Ibid.*, p. 53
15. *Ibid.*, p. 142
16. Wallace Stevens, *Collected Poems*, p. 19

Chapter VII: Documents and Correspondences

1. Richard Seaver, Terry Southern, and Alexander Trocchi, eds., *Writers in Revolt*, p. 155
2. Quoted in Jerome Rothenberg's *Technicians of the Sacred*, p. 490
3. Eugene Jolas, ed., *transition Workshop*, p. 173
4. Ernest Fenollosa, *The Chinese Written Character as a Medium for Poetry*, p. 17

5. Edward Sapir in Benjamin Whorf, *Language, Thought, and Reality*, p. 134
6. D. H. Lawrence, *Fantasia of the Unconscious*, p. 114
7. Gertrude Stein, *Bee Time Vine*, p. 55
8. Claude Lévi-Strauss, *Structural Anthropology*, p. 198
9. William Burroughs and Brion Gysin, *The Exterminator*, p. 5
10. Wittgenstein quoted in David Antin's *Definitions*, p. 33
11. Daniel Breslaw in David Ebin, ed., *The Drug Experience*, p. 336
12. Harry Stack Sullivan, *Schizophrenia as Human Process*, p. 61
13. Marshall McLuhan, "The Reversal of the Overheated Image," *Playboy*, Jan., 1968
14. Clark Coolidge, "Poems," *Paris Review* No. 43, Summer 1968
15. Paul Carroll, ed., *The Young American Poets*, p. 149
16. Aram Saroyan, *Copyright 1968 by Aram Saroyon*. Mr. Saroyan's book consists of a wrapped ream of typewriter paper with the first sheet reading COPYRIGHT 1968 by Aram Saroyan. In conversation Mr. Saroyan told me that the U.S. copyright office refused to copyright it
17. Lewis Welch, *On Out*. No page nos.
18. Robert Kelly, *Finding the Measure* p. 49
19. Jerome Rothenberg, "Rattle for Baby I," *some/thing* magazine, no. II, Winter, 1965, p. 48
20. Jackson McLow, "Friendship Poems," *Ibid.*, p. 58
21. Robert Duncan, The Opening of the Field, p. 12

Bibliography

Antin, David. *Definitions*. New York: Caterpillar Press, 1967.

Beckett, Samuel, and Sixteen Other Authors. *Our Exagmination Around His Factification of Incamnation of Work in Progress*. London: Faber and Faber, 1929.

Boas, Francis. *Language, Race, Culture*. New York: Holt, Rinehart, 1918.

Boyle, Kay and McAlmon, Robert. *Being Geniuses Together*. New York: Doubleday, 1967.

Breton, André. *Manifesto of Surrealism*. University of Michigan Press, 1969.

Briere, Eugene John. *A Psycholinguistic Study of Phonological Interference*. The Hague, Netherlands: Mouton, 1968.

Brinnin, John Malcolm. *The Third Rose: Gertrude Stein and Her World*. Boston: Little Brown, 1959.

Brown, Norman O. *Life Against Death*. New York: Random House, 1959.

———. *Love's Body*. New York: Random House, 1966.

Burroughs, William S. *The Exterminator*. San Francisco: Haselwood Books, 1960.

————. *Naked Lunch*. New York: Grove Press, 1959.

————. *The Ticket That Exploded*. New York: Grove Press, 1967.

Cage, John. *Silence*. Middletown, Connecticut: Wesleyan University Press, 1961.

————. *A Year From Monday*. Middletown, Connecticut: Wesleyan University Press, 1967.

Carroll, John B. *Language and Thought*. New York: Prentice-Hall, 1964.

Carroll, Paul, ed. *The Young American Poets*. Chicago: Follett, 1968.

Chomsky, Noam. *Syntactic Structures*. The Hague, Netherlands: Mouton, 1967.

Church, Joseph. *Language and the Discovery of Reality*. New York: Random House, 1961.

Davie, Donald. *Articulate Energy—An Inquiry Into the Syntax of English Poetry*. London: Routledge and Kegan Paul, 1955.

Duncan, Robert. *The Opening of the Field*. New York: Grove Press, 1961.

————. *Writing, writing*. Buffalo, New York: Sunbooks, 1964.

Ebin, David, ed. *The Drug Experience*. New York: Orion Press, 1961.

Fenollosa, Ernest. *The Chinese Written Character as a Medium for Poetry*. San Francisco: City Lights, 1961.

Gibson, Walker, ed. *The Limits of Language*. New York: Hill and Wang, 1962.

Goldstein, Richard. *The Poetry of Rock*. New York: Bantam Books, 1969.

Hassan, Ihab. *The Literature of Silence: Henry Miller and Samuel Beckett*. New York: Alfred A. Knopf, 1967.

Hoffman, Michael J. *The Development of Abstractionism in the Writings of Gertrude Stein*. Philadelphia: The University of Pennsylvania Press, 1965.

Hornblow, Arthur and Leonora. *Animals Do the Strangest Things*. New York: Random House, 1964.

Jackson, Holbrook, ed. *The Complete Nonsense of Edward Lear*. New York: Dover Publications, 1961.

Jacobovitz, Leon A. and Miron, Murray, eds. *Readings in the Psychology of Language*. New Jersey: Prentice-Hall, 1967.

James, William. *The Principles of Psychology*. 1890. Reprint. New York: Dover Publications, 1950.

Jolas, Eugene, ed. *transition Workshop*. New York: Vanguard Press, 1949.

Joyce, James. *Finnegans Wake*. New York: Viking Press, 1939.

Kasanin, J. S. *Language and Thought in Schizophrenia*. New York: Norton, 1964.

Kelly, Robert. *Finding the Measure*. Los Angeles: Black Sparrow Press, 1968.

————, and Leary, T., eds. *A Controversy of Poets*. New York: Doubleday, 1965.

Krauss, Ruth. *There's a little ambiguity over there among the bluebells*. New York: Something Else Press, 1968.

Laing, R. D. *The Divided Self*. London: Penguin Books, 1965.

————. *The Politics of Experience*. New York: Ballantine Books, 1968.

Lawrence, D. H. *Fantasia of the Unconscious*. New York: Viking Press, 1960.

Lee, Irving. *The Language of Wisdom and Folly*. New York: Harper, 1947.

Lévi-Strauss, Claude. *Structural Anthropology*. New York: Basic Books, 1963.

Lewis, R. W. B. *The American Adam*. Chicago: The University of Chicago Press, 1961.

McLuhan, Marshall. *The Gutenberg Galaxy*. Toronto: University of Toronto Press, 1962.

————. *The Mechanical Bride*. New York: Vanguard Press, 1951.

————. "The Reversal of the Overheated Image." *Playboy*, December, 1968, p. 133.

————. *Understanding Media*. New York: Signet Books, 1964.

Marks, Elaine, ed. *French Poetry From Baudelaire to the Present*. New York: Dell, 1962.

Marleau-Ponty, Maurice. "Cézanne's Doubt." *Art and Literature* #23, Belgium.

————. *The Primacy of Perception*. New York: Basic Books, 1957.

Nadeau, Maurice. *The History of Surrealism*. New York: Macmillan, 1965.

Newell, William Wells. *Games and Songs of American Children*. New York: Dover Publications, 1965.

Piaget, Jean. *The Language and Thought of the Child*. New York: Meridian Books, 1955.

Porter, Katherine Anne. *The Days Before*. New York: Harcourt Brace, 1952.

Pound, Ezra. *ABC of Reading*. New York: New Directions, 1960.

Rabkin, Leslie Y., ed. *Psychopathology and Literature*. San Francisco: Chandler Publishers, 1966.

Reid, B. L. *Art By Subtraction: A Dissenting Opinion of Gertrude Stein*. Norman, Okla.: The University of Oklahoma Press, 1958.

Rexroth, Kenneth. *Assays*. New York: New Directions, 1961.

———. *Birds in the Bush*. New York: New Directions, 1959.

Riding, Laura. "Gertrude Stein and the New Barbarism," *transition #3*, June 1927.

Rosenblum, Robert. *Cubism and the Twentieth Century*. New York: Abrams, n.d.

Rothenberg, Jerome. *Technicians of the Sacred*. New York: Doubleday, 1968.

Sapir, Edward. *Language*. New York: Harcourt Brace, 1921.

Saporta, Sol., ed. *Psycholinguistics*. New York: Holt, Rinehart, 1961.

Saroyan, Aram. *Copyright 1968 by Aram Saroyan*. New York: Kulchur Press, 1968.

Seaver, Richard, Southern, Terry and Trocchi, Alexander, eds. *Writers in Revolt*. New York: Frederick Pell, 1963.

Skinner, B. F. "Has Gertrude Stein a Secret?" *Atlantic,* no. 153, January 1934, p. 53.

Stein, Gertrude. *Alphabets and Birthdays*. New Haven, Connecticut: Yale University Press, 1957.

———. As Fine As Melanctha. New Haven, Connecticut: Yale University Press, 1954.

———. Bee Time Vine. New Haven, Connecticut: Yale University Press, 1953.

———. "Cultivated Motor Automatism: A Study of Character in its Relation to Attention," Harvard Psychological Review, no. 3, 1898, pp. 295–306.

———. *Geography and Plays*. New York: Something Else Press, 1968.

———. How to Write. Paris: Plain Editions, 1931.

———. *Lectures in America*. Boston: Beacon Press, 1959.

———. *Lucy Church Amiably*. New York: Something Else Press, 1969.

———. *The Making of Americans*. New York: Something Else Press, 1967.

————. *Mrs. Reynolds and Five Earlier Novelettes*. New Haven, Connecticut: Yale University Press, 1952.

————. with Leon Solomons. "Normal Motor Automatism." *Harvard Psychological Review*, 1896, pp. 492–512.

————. *Picasso*. Boston: Beacon Press, 1959.

————. *Portraits & Prayers*. New York: Random House, 1934.

————. *Selected Writings*, ed. by Carl Van Vechten. New York: Modern Library, 1962.

————. *Stanzas in Meditation*. New Haven, Connecticut: Yale University Press, 1956.

————. *Three Lives*. New York: Random House, 1961.

————. *The World Is Round*. New York: William Scott, 1939.

Stevens, Wallace. *Collected Poems*. New York: Alfred A. Knopf, 1959.

Steward, Allegra. *Gertrude Stein and the Present*. Cambridge, Mass.: Harvard University Press, 1967.

Sullivan, Harry Stack. *Schizophrenia as a Human Process*. New York: Norton, 1962.

Sutherland, Donald. *Gertrude Stein: A Biography of Her Work*. New Haven, Connecticut, Yale University Press, 1951.

Toklas, Alice B. *What Is Remembered*. New York: Holt, Rinehart, 1963.

Welch, Lewis. Unpublished undergraduate thesis on Gertrude Stein. Reed College, Department of Language and Literature, Portland Oregon, 1950.

————. *On Out*. Oyez, Berkeley, California, 1967.

Whorf, Benjamin Lee. *Language, Thought and Reality*. Cambridge, Massachusetts: M.I.T. Press, 1964.

Williams, William Carlos. *Selected Essays*. New York: New Directions, 1954.

Wilson, Edmund. *Axel's Castle*. New York: Charles Scribners, 1931.

Index

Three Fables (Flaubert), 17
Three Lives (Stein), 8, 16, 17, 24, 25, 28, 31, 32, 39, 40, 45, 91, 107
Ticket That Exploded, The (Burroughs), 114
Time, tension between actual and narrative, 37–38
Toklas, Alice B., 75, 94, 113, 116
transition, little magazine, 57, 107
Tristram Shandy (Sterns), 72
Tzara, Tristan, 56, 57, 104–6

Ulysses (Joyce), 19
"Un Coup de des . . ." (Mallarmé), 48, 49

Valéry, Paul, 3, 4, 5, 76
Van Vechten, Carl, 57, 129
Varieties of Religious Experience (James), 97
Verb tense, Miss Stein's play with, 42
Verbal games: of children, 53–54, 66–67; use of, in *Four Saints in Three Acts*, 76–77, 78
Verbosity of Miss Stein, 30
Verlaine, Paul, 3
"Vibratory syntax" of Miss Stein, 87–88, 93
Visionary writer, Miss Stein as, 109–10
Vitalism of James and Whitehead, 90
Vocabulary, Miss Stein's use of a simple and straightforward, 52

Waiting for Godot (Beckett), 79
Welch, Lewis, 122

Whitehead, Alfred North, 57, 88, 90, 94, 114
Whitman, Walt, 4, 13
Whorf, Benjamin, 6, 52, 109, 113, 114
Wilder, Thornton, 57, 91
Williams, William Carlos, 66, 67, 129
Wilson, Edmund, 3, 9, 28, 37
Wittgenstein, Ludwig, 47, 57, 114–15, 128
Woolf, Virginia, 15
Words: positional flexibility of, in Miss Stein's personal grammar, 43–44; as discrete semantic carriers, Miss Stein's abandonment of, 44–45; conventional word organization, 44; word magic, 53–56; word play of children, 53–54, 66–67; Miss Stein's use of, 56, 60; melody of, 66; verbal games in *Four Saints in Three Acts*, 76–77, 78; Miss Stein's technique of placing equal perceptual stress on perception of, 85–86; revolution of, 103–8, 128; rhythm and play of, 110–11; shamanism, and power of, 112–13
Wordworth, William, 87
World Is Round, The (Stein), 110
World of political and social responsibilities, Miss Stein's indifference toward, 75
Wright, Richard, 28

Yeats, W. B., 104

Zola, Émile, 90